MW00461158

'A gem. Pierre Hazan's elegant introduction to mediating in armed conflict catches both the art and the moral dilemmas of modern peace making.'

David Harland, Executive Director of the
Centre for Humanitarian Dialogue

'Fast paced in style yet profound in substance, this is an important book and also an excellent read ... Hazan deals with the troublesome complexities in an admirably clear way. It deserves the widest audience—not just among experts and practitioners, but among general readers too. Hazan's learning, experiences and style of writing means both groups will be amply rewarded.'

Andrew Gilmour, former UN Assistant Secretary General
for Human Rights

'Analyses with finesse what this quest for dialogue means in an increasingly chaotic world where the West is no longer hegemonic.'

Le Monde

'Lifts the veil on the dilemmas and pitfalls of mediation in armed conflicts.'

Le Figaro

'Revisits the last thirty years in the theatre of mass crimes from Bosnia to the Sahel, from Ukraine to Afghanistan.'

Libération

'An enlightening and stimulating book on mediation in armed conflicts.'

Le Temps

'Former journalist, and now advisor to the Centre for Humanitarian Dialogue in Geneva, Pierre Hazan has written *Negotiating with the Devil*. In this stimulating opus, the author examines mediation in times of war.'

Le Croix

'An enlightening book on [Hazan's] experience as a mediator in armed conflicts.'

Le Pèlerin

'An engrossing look at the moral dilemmas and shifting political imperatives in conflict mediation. With his usual uncompromising honesty and drawing on his rich personal experience as a mediator, Hazan eschews easy answers and bright lines in considering when to talk with the most evil forces, and when compromise and neutrality can become complicity.'

Reed Brody, author of *To Catch a Dictator*

'Peace or Justice? Engagement or sanctions? Neutrality or impartiality? Such critical dilemmas animate this fascinating book about conflict mediation in which Hazan draws from his significant field experiences to offer fresh answers.'

Ruti Teitel, Director of the Institute for Global Law, Justice and Policy, author of *Globalizing Transitional Justice*

'Hazan plunges the reader into the fray of conflicts, in search of possible links bringing warring parties together. Far from a heroic account, based on long experience in the field, he exposes the harsh dilemmas and necessary compromises of a little known action.'

Rony Brauman, former president of Médecins Sans Frontières, and author of *Humanitarian Wars?: Lies and Brainwashing*

NEGOTIATING WITH THE DEVIL

PIERRE HAZAN
with the collaboration of
Emmanuelle Hazan

Negotiating with the Devil

*Inside the World of
Armed Conflict Mediation*

Translated by
Susan Mutti

HURST & COMPANY, LONDON

First published in the United Kingdom in 2024 by
C. Hurst & Co. (Publishers) Ltd.,
New Wing, Somerset House, Strand, London WC2R 1LA
Copyright © Pierre Hazan, 2024
English translation © Susan Mutti
All rights reserved.

Distributed in the United States, Canada and Latin America by
Oxford University Press, 198 Madison Avenue, New York, NY 10016,
United States of America.

A Cataloguing-in-Publication data record for this book
is available from the British Library.

ISBN: 9781911723110

This book is printed using paper from registered sustainable
and managed sources.

www.hurstpublishers.com

Printed in Great Britain by Bell and Bain Ltd, Glasgow

In memory of my parents.

'War is father of all and king of all'
Heraclitus, Fragments, 31.53

CONTENTS

Acknowledgements   xv
Preface to the English Edition   xvii

PART ONE
IN THE FOG OF THE PEACE PROCESS

1. Exploring Grey Areas   3
2. Should We Negotiate with the Devil?   17
3. From Morality to Hubris   29
4. To Negotiate or Not to Negotiate?   41
5. The End of Pax Americana   53

PART TWO
IN SEARCH OF THE LESSER EVIL

6. From Compromise to Complicity?   67
7. Neutrality in the Face of Genocide   81
8. Bosnia: Farewell to Neutrality   95
9. Syria: Mission Impossible   111

CONTENTS

10. The Sahel: Talking with Jihadists   127
Conclusion: The Deregulation of Force   145

Notes   157
Further Reading   181
Index   185

ACKNOWLEDGEMENTS

This book would not have been possible without the support of the Robert Bosch Foundation and the months I spent in Berlin working on the manuscript. In particular, I would like to thank the Foundation's Senior Vice-President Henry Alt-Haaker, Léonie Schaefer-Osthues and Antonio Fox, and the other fellows at the Robert Bosch Academy for the many fascinating exchanges we had during my stay there.

I would also like to thank David Lanz and Antoine Garapon for reading the manuscript and for their sage advice, and Mathieu Pellerin for his perspective as an expert on the Sahel.

This book is the fruit of countless conversations spanning years with too many people for me to name. May they be thanked here. At the risk of forgetting many of them, I would like to address a special word of thanks to David Harland, director of the Centre for Humanitarian Dialogue, whose very British sense of humour and enlightening conversations I have always found stimulating, and to my other colleagues, including David Gorman,

ACKNOWLEDGEMENTS

Romain Grandjean, Katia Papagianni, Alexandre Liebeskind, Béatrice Mégevand, Babatunde Afolabi, Liza Rekthman and the Sviatohirsk group in the Donbas, Sandra Petrovic, Kiari Moustapha and her colleagues in Diffa (Niger), and Kader Sidibe, Freddy Nkurkiye and their respective teams in the Sahel and Central Africa.

I also wish to thank Mark Freeman and all my colleagues at the Law and Practice Group of the Institute for Integrated Transitions for all the discussions we have had over the past few years, along with Gilad Ben Nun and Reed Brody. Last but not least, my thanks also go to Brian Currin and the other members of the International Contact Group on the Basque Conflict, and to Gorka Espiau.

I have a heartfelt thought for the courage and moral rectitude of the late Monsignor Jean-Louis Nahimana, President of the Truth and Reconciliation Commission of Burundi, with whom I travelled through his country and who sought to discharge his mandate despite all the obstacles.

My deepest thanks also go to my children, Ilan, Chaya, Nora and Sam, who from a very young age taught me a great deal about negotiation and mediation.

PREFACE TO THE ENGLISH EDITION

As the English edition of this book was about to go to press, I decided to add a brief, last-minute preface related to the war between Israel and Hamas, while events were still unfolding.

On 21 November 2023, Qatar, with the support of Egypt and the United States, mediated an unprecedented agreement between the two belligerents, locked in an all-out war. This mediation struck me as emblematic of today's worrying trends, in both the terms of the agreement and the nature of the mediator. It reflects blatant contempt for the laws of war and it highlights the United Nations' total impotence. Most importantly, it is led by a mediator underwriting one of the parties—which has been qualified as a 'terrorist organisation' by the UN.

Welcome to a multipolar world where deals of this kind may be in the protagonists' short-term interests but do not make them any less determined to eradicate their adversary.

The chain of events during this brief period is as follows. On 7 October 2023, Hamas launched a surprise attack, massacring some one thousand Israeli civilians and abducting 240 people, including children, women and elderly people. The Israeli army retaliated with brutal reprisals, targeting Hamas but causing the deaths of 14,000 Palestinians in Gaza, including 5,000 children. Six weeks later, the two parties agreed on the following points: at least 50 hostages, women and children held by Hamas, would gradually be released in exchange for 150 Palestinian women and children incarcerated in Israel, the releases to take place over the course of a four-day cease-fire. The parties no doubt also discussed guarantees that Hamas's political leaders would not be the subject of targeted killings but the outcome of those discussions is unknown. The central fact remains: the agreement constitutes a scathing rebuttal of all those who claim, 'We do not negotiate with terrorists'.

It is the terms of this unprecedented agreement that are so astounding: the release of around fifty hostages was essentially to be paid for in days of cease-fire. There would be an extra day of cease-fire for every ten additional hostages released. In other words, and in purely theoretical terms, for each hostage released beyond the original group, Hamas will 'gain' 2 hours and 40 minutes of cease-fire—a startling calculation whereby the 'price' of releasing hostages is expressed as a prolongation of the pause in the fighting. Hamas wants the truce to last as long as possible in order to reorganise and heighten the political and media pressure on the Israeli government to end its military intervention in Gaza. It agreed to the deal because it believed that what it stood to gain by releasing the hostages outweighed the military advantage of prolonging the hostilities.

The deal is also unusual, if not unique, in that an elected authority (Hamas was elected to govern Gaza in 2006, in elections deemed 'regular' by the European Union) considered it legitimate to take women and children as hostages. Under Article 8(2) of the Rome Statute of the International Criminal Court—which Palestine has ratified—hostage-taking constitutes a war crime. That said, little more than lip service is paid to international humanitarian law in this region and the results of the Court's inquiries into past allegations on both sides remain pending.

Last but not least, Qatar's mediation is a crystal clear example of the end of Western hegemony over the international system. A tiny emirate pursues a high-stakes diplomatic policy for its own benefit. It makes itself useful to the Israelis while sheltering the political leaders of an organisation that the United Nations and the West qualify as 'terrorist'. Indeed, Qatar is Hamas's main donor and protector and at the same time Washington's strategic partner and home to the largest American military base in the region. It has never condemned the 7 October attacks against Israeli civilians but describes the Israeli response as war crimes ... which in no way prevented it from simultaneously welcoming the head of

Mossad and Israeli diplomats to negotiate the hostages' release. What is more, Qatar owns Al Jazeera, a media conglomerate with an editorial line in Arabic that is close to that of Hamas and stakes in some of the largest Western companies ... and a prestigious football club, Paris Saint-Germain. Nor is this Qatar's first brush with international diplomacy: together with Egypt, it helped organise previous cease-fires between Israel and Hamas.

This latest example shows the extent of the changes sweeping the field of mediation in a multipolar world. Beyond Qatar, who would have imagined that Saudi Arabia and the United Arab Emirates would get involved some time earlier in prisoner exchanges between Russia and Ukraine? That China would profile itself as a mediating power in the Middle East and seal the re-establishment of ties between Tehran and Riyadh?[1]

The world has entered what Samir Saran, president of the Indian think tank Observer Research Foundation, calls 'limited liability partnerships'[2], which consist in arrangements and structures (regional organisations, coalitions, various pacts) that may even sometimes compete with each other. This 'minilateralism' is a form of constantly shifting multilateralism on the cheap in which each party seeks to maximise its short-term interest, at the risk of sparking a violent reaction from those excluded from its agreements. The violence of the Hamas attack on 7 October must therefore be understood in the light of the process of normalisation between the Gulf monarchies and Israel, in which scant attention was paid to the plight of the Palestinians. Of course, the world we once knew was also driven by clearly understood State interests. But the relative stability of the international environment meant that any agreements concluded had a more solid foundation.

A multipolar world encourages pragmatism: here or there, the enemy can, for a time and on a given subject, be a partner. Such purely transactional agreements only last as long as deemed appropriate by the parties. Thus, despite the violence of the fighting, Russia and Ukraine signed an agreement on the export of cereals on July 22, 2022, following mediation by Turkey and the United Nations. They extended the agreement twice before the Kremlin chose not to renew it a year later, ultimately judging that Ukraine benefited more than it did.

Arrangements of this kind reflect a fundamental change: the end of Western hegemony is weakening international institutions and the standards put in place over the last thirty years (which the European and American governments were far from always observing). This development presents as much danger as opportunity. In this era of uncertainty, the precautionary principle prevails in its most basic form: everyone is arming to the teeth, and quickly. Global military expenditure hit a new record in 2022, with European spending rising to levels not seen in at least thirty years.[3] However, neither the pragmatism of minilateralism nor the new arms race is of the slightest use in meeting the global challenges we face.

We have to build a new international architecture of security, reduce the inequalities that are the wellsprings of tension and violence, and above all face up to the climate transition, with more than three billion people living in 'highly vulnerable' regions. We therefore need to reconstruct what is so sorely lacking today: a shared ethos. In the meantime, mediations will be conducted with all kind of armed actors, in the knowledge that all the protagonists may well see the devil in each other.

Pierre Hazan, 23 November 2023

PART ONE

IN THE FOG OF THE PEACE PROCESS

1

EXPLORING GREY AREAS

Autumn 1993. Bosnia-Herzegovina is at war. I was a journalist reporting—as truthfully as possible, in and of itself no mean feat—on the ongoing violence and abuse. The search for truth was no easy task in the Balkans, where no side held a monopoly on war crimes. I wrapped myself in the 'ethics of conviction', the philosophy that my actions could remain faithful to my ideas. The ethics of conviction made me a fact-finder, gave coherence to my work and exempted me, at least partly, from its consequences.

While covering a story near Mostar, I found myself in a situation that forced me to temporarily drop the ethics of conviction and bear witness to, even play a modest role in, a process of human selection. I had been 'embedded' in a team of humanitarian workers that was given an unexpected task: to decide who should be released from a grim detention camp. International pressure had had at least some positive effects: a third of the 2,000 or so prisoners being held were to be released. But now it was up to us to choose who would go free, knowing that those who were not released faced death. The conditions in the camp were terrible, the men packed together on the floor of a shed that had been hollowed out of a cliff and once used as a munitions dump by the Yugoslav army. The men lived in fetid semi-darkness, with almost no time outdoors.

To identify the weakest among the prisoners, we brought in scales and measuring tapes and began calculating each prisoner's body mass index. One of us took the detainees' measurements; a second weighed them; a third, seated at a small wooden table, wrote down the numbers. The prisoners had lost 20 to 30 kg each, sometimes more. We took turns, changing places every half hour. Explosions could be heard in the distance. The front line was only a dozen kilometres away. Some of the guards and prisoners had been schoolmates, growing up and playing together as children.

I have told this story elsewhere,[1] but in that previous telling I did not mention something that prompted me to write this book: my impression that the belligerents had won a moral victory by forcing a team of humanitarian workers to engage in such a degrading act of human selection. Who among the prisoners would we free? To what extent should we compromise our ethical principles by participating in the selection of who would or would not be saved?

Our contact in the camp, Berislav Pušić, a stout, unpleasant man, had a function I had never heard of: a senior official of the Bosnian Croat wartime entity Herceg-Bosna, he was in charge of prisoner exchanges. I quickly realised that he had worked out a true *modus operandi*, becoming, in his own way, an expert in his chosen field. He gauged the value of his prisoners according to their occupation, family connections, even whether or not they had cousins in Germany, Austria or Switzerland who might be willing to pay for their release. He was ready to give up only those prisoners he considered worthless (i.e. poor), selling the others to the opposing side or in some other financial deal. Should we accept his terms to save as many lives as possible, at the risk of entering into a dangerous logic of submission? On the other hand, if we stuck to our principles and insisted on evacuating the weakest, we risked jeopardising the negotiations and preventing any release at all. What should we do? Opinions within the team differed. The legal advisor wanted to hold fast to principles, fearing that 'giving in to blackmail' would open the door to future manipulation. The head of operations retorted that human lives were worth more than the purity of principles. In my heart, I wavered between one position and the other. Our dilemma found its own tragic answer: the officer in charge of prisoner exchanges decided suddenly that there would be no releases. None at all. A dozen buses that had been parked in front of the camp, waiting to take hundreds of prisoners to freedom, drove away, empty.

During those few days, I realised how burdensome the 'ethics of responsibility'—the pragmatic search to adjust the means to the end—could be, and the potentially fatal consequences that might arise as a result. The members of the humanitarian team were of the highest integrity. One of them, a doctor, kept saying he did not want to become 'another Mengele', voicing aloud the questions and fears we all had. How could we do the least harm? For my part, I felt dirty, sullied by the belligerents' cynicism and the madness of war. The line between good and evil was suddenly blurred. I had the feeling that, here and elsewhere, the belligerents were taking a perverse pleasure in forcing the United Nations (UN), the International Committee of the Red Cross (ICRC) and others to bear witness to, even to underwrite, their 'cattle market', where prisoners, tobacco, oil, petrol and human remains were sometimes all part of the same 'deal'. These men were ready to kill each other, yet understood each other perfectly when it came to haggling over goods. The lives of a few poor souls were just one more commodity in their sordid barter.

It was a source of cold comfort when I saw the very same senior official of Herceg-Bosna, Berislav Pušić, twenty-four years later, in the dock at the International Criminal Tribunal for the former Yugoslavia (ICTY) and watched as he was sentenced to ten years in prison for war crimes and crimes against humanity.[2] In an electrifying turn of events, one of his co-defendants, Slobodan Praljak, a Croatian general and former theatre director, stood up to hear his sentence and swallowed a phial of poison in front of the stunned judges, committing suicide right before their eyes, and the eyes of the public, for the trial was televised.[3] With that dramatic development, the first UN international criminal tribunal wound up its work.

The situation I experienced in that camp in autumn 1993 raised questions about the responsibility, both political and moral, of third parties seeking to mitigate, if they cannot end, the suffering caused by war. It is that role, of the mediator, with all the ambiguities of the job, that is the subject of this book. I hope posing these questions will better equip others to make choices fraught with consequences.

* * *

Some fifteen years later, I became involved in mediation as a member of the International Contact Group on the Basque Conflict. Then, in 2014, I joined an organisation that mediates in armed conflicts, the Centre for Humanitarian Dialogue. Now, it was my turn to confront the ethics of responsibility and difficult choices. I felt a certain irony in finding myself in this position. As a journalist, I had been close to human rights activists and their thirst for justice, and to criminal proceedings against perpetrators of mass crimes. I had accompanied Reed Brody of Human Rights Watch on one of his missions to N'Djamena, Chad, and together we had found the archives of that country's political police and of its government's reign of terror, which would prove decisive in enabling the trial of the former president and dictator Hissène Habré. The trial was historic: for the first time, the African Union had created a special court, the Extraordinary African Chambers, to try a former head of state for war crimes, crimes against humanity, and even the rapes that Habré had himself committed. Now, after leaving journalism and the UN, where I was briefly political adviser to the High Commissioner for Human Rights, I found myself inside peace processes, having to speak courteously with people I had once reviled with my pen. I participated in the drafting of an amnesty law for members of an armed group, a far cry from my previous career denouncing their crimes.

The search for peace had taken precedence over the search for justice. I abandoned the ethics of conviction and the denunciation of war criminals for the ethics of responsibility. The ethics of conviction, being on the side of good, no longer satisfied me; it seemed detached from the need to face the reality of an international community made up of pragmatists and unsatisfactory compromises. From now on, acting in accordance with my conscience would mean walking a tightrope between cynical pragmatism and naive optimism, both of which are counterproductive. Peace is a messy, chaotic business, as is the road that leads to it. In the peace process, as in war, everything is negotiable, down to the distribution of ministerial posts and the ranks of the militiamen incorporated into the army at the end of the hostilities.

As a mediator in armed conflicts, I specialised in one of the field's most ethically sensitive points: issues of justice, amnesty and reparation. I dealt with the same representatives of governments and armed groups who had committed war crimes and who were determined to escape any punishment, even if that meant more conflict and bloodshed. The challenge for me was to identify what little leeway there was to keep the peace process moving, to lay the groundwork for the eventual establishment of the rule of law, and to give as much satisfaction as possible to the victims.

In his book of essays, *The Drowned and the Saved*, Auschwitz survivor Primo Levi evokes 'the grey zone', that 'poorly defined' troubled and ambiguous area in which 'the two camps of masters and servants both diverge and converge' and which 'contains within itself enough to confuse our need to judge'.[4] Peace processes also have a grey zone—fortunately less tragic—between the belligerents, for whom the end justifies the means, and the mediators and humanitarians who, with different approaches and goals, try to limit the suffering. Can we advance in this grey zone, walk this razor's edge, 'saving bodies so that the future remains possible', as Albert Camus once said,[5] without losing our soul, without slipping from compromise into complicity? To what point can we remain neutral between aggressors and the aggressed? I have struggled with this Faustian pact time and again since I began working in armed-conflict mediation.

The need for a moral compass

To work in conflict resolution is to accept penetrating into the fog that is the search for peace, that grey zone where enemies may find points of convergence despite conflicting interests. I long ago abandoned the comfort of the ethics of conviction, the luxury of being consistent with myself, to shoulder the ethics of responsibility and focus on encouraging compromise and pragmatism, depending on the case, to reach the desired end.

The ethics of responsibility is not without risk for mediators. There is the risk of being manipulated, that the promised peace will turn out to be an illusion, like the Munich Agreement of 1938, merely a truce before the outbreak of something worse; or that it will itself sow the seeds of a new bloody conflict; or that the 'peace' is built on the backs of other people, as in the case of the German–Soviet Nonaggression Pact concluded between Hitler and Stalin to carve up Poland and the Baltic states. There is also the risk that the mediators' determination to pursue the peace process in the face of the parties' mounting radicalisation becomes counterproductive to the point that it exacerbates the conflict. This happened with the Norwegian mediation between the Sri Lankan government and the Liberation Tigers of Tamil Eelam (LTTE, better known as the Tamil Tigers). The Sri Lankan army used the final talks as a smokescreen to deceive their enemy and crush it by force of arms.[6]

There is also the risk that mediation will lend legitimacy to armed groups terrorising civilians or marginalise those who oppose them non-violently. In the heat of the moment, it is no easy task to pick the lesser evil: by participating in the displacement of civilians in Syria are you saving them from death or playing into the hands of a policy of demographic engineering? Depending on the point of view, the same action can be interpreted as preserving thousands of lives or as a criminal act subject to prosecution.

One mediator confided to me that he had once tossed a coin to decide whether an agreed exchange of prisoners, which he was overseeing, could take place or not. The prisoners had been waiting for hours in buses on both sides of the front line, many holding their heads in their hands, uncertain of the fate awaiting them. Not all of the conditions set out for the exchange had been met, including and above all for the prisoners' security. The risk was great that it could all go very wrong, that with one misconstrued move the situation could blow up. On the other hand, should the mediator compromise the freedom of these men? Weighing the pros and cons, unable to bear the responsibility of a call made in the face of too many unknowns, he delegated the decision to Fate, tossing a coin: heads prison; tails freedom. This frightening story spoke volumes to me, because it illustrated how extremely difficult it is for mediators to make decisions with the fate of men, women and children hanging in the balance, based not only on reason, but also on intuition and wild bets. Like war, peace involves the balance of power, strategic considerations and political goals—a condition that, in my view, forces mediators to reflect on the limitations and impact of their actions. It is this grey zone that I wanted to explore to help other mediators.

I wrote this book to set out, in the light of experience, a method or at least some basic principles to lower the risk that mediation is corrupted and to ensure that decisions are not being taken on a roll of the dice, the toss of a coin.

After a decade in this obscure world, that process wherein a third party assists belligerents, with their accord, to prevent, manage or resolve conflict, I felt the need to re-examine the dilemmas and questions that have arisen during peace processes from Bosnia-Herzegovina to Syria, from Mali to Colombia, in Ukraine and in many other places. What is the mediator's responsibility when two belligerents conclude a peace agreement to the detriment of a third party? To what extent should mediators participate in 'ethnic cleansing'—even if what they might do could save lives? Is achieving a fragile peace worth sacrificing justice—or will that sacrifice merely fuel a new cycle of violence? In this book I aim to map out the most dangerous ethical areas and dilemmas facing mediators and to set some benchmarks. My objective, no doubt too ambitious, is to help provide a moral compass for mediators in a world of violent and constant change.

A genealogy of the 'enemies of humankind'

Mediators work within the geopolitical environment and norms shaped by the balance of power between major players on the international stage. In Greek mythology, killing the Minotaur makes Theseus a hero of civilisation, like Heracles, who purged the lands of brigands and monsters. The mythological Minotaur is the incarnation of an evil that exacts a heavy toll on humans. From time immemorial, societies have used such symbols to personify the dark shadow within human nature, this obstruction to an idea of human good; our era is no exception. The first part of the book examines how evil has been given a 'face' in the West since the end of the Cold War, and the impact this personification has had on the search for peace. Can any realistic peace process exclude 'war criminals' and 'terrorists' while at the same time including military and political 'leaders'? My book examines the ambiguity in this dialectic and how it has constantly evolved and been reconfigured over the past three decades.

In this respect, I consider three successive periods. First, the moment in the 1990s when the Kantian dream of peace took shape: that of international justice in a time of war, the hope that international tribunals would curb violence by prosecuting war criminals in the midst of a conflict. The tension created by this search for peace and justice continues, even today, in Ukraine.

Then, with the attacks of 11 September 2001 and the reaction of the US government, another ideal emerged: that of a war on terror that would purge the world of 'terrorists'. This period, too, saw the introduction of international norms and anti-terrorist policies, at the risk of compounding war by war in a binary vision. Here, too, I examine the contradictions between, on the one hand, a policy of criminalising/eliminating 'terrorist organisations' and, on the other, the goal of mediation to end wars; thus, the need to deal with those who are excluded from the peace process, from Afghanistan to the Sahel, via the Middle East. In particular, we will see how some European governments outsource dialogue with 'terrorists' to private mediation organisations in an attempt to extricate themselves from a hole of their own digging.

Lastly, I review the most recent period, from the war in Syria to the hostilities in Ukraine, and consider how the West's loss of hegemony is reshaping the space for mediation. This period is marked by the deregulation of force in a now multipolar world, by the resurgence of geopolitical confrontation and by the rejection of norms that the West once held to be universal, even if it did not always respect them itself, as evidenced by the invasion of Iraq in 2003.

I aim, also, to demonstrate the inadequacies of the war on terror and of international criminal justice in time of war, two failures that make it all the more urgent to carve out a space for mediation. This urgency obliges mediators to avoid falling into the trap of hyper-pragmatism, whereby, on the pretext that it is sometimes necessary to deal with perpetrators of terrible crimes, any and all acts can be permitted. The obligation to maintain a moral structure is critical, including, if not especially, in borderline situations.

This is the subject of the second part of the book, where I explore the dialectic of inclusion/exclusion of war criminals and 'terrorists', this time at the level of mediators confronted with borderline situations in an increasingly multipolar and fragmented world. I start with the internal debates of the ICRC on the definition of neutrality during the genocide of the Second World War and go on to examine how the United Nations came to abandon this concept of neutrality in the aftermath of the Srebrenica massacres. Finally, I examine two contemporary conflicts: the moral dilemmas facing the mediators in Syria struggling to protect populations, and the ongoing debate about mediation with armed jihadist groups in the Sahel region of North Africa.

2

SHOULD WE NEGOTIATE WITH THE DEVIL?

On 3 April 2022, during a press conference in Warsaw, Polish Prime Minister Mateusz Morawiecki harshly rebuked French President Emmanuel Macron, who had met sixteen times with Vladimir Putin since the start of the year in the hope of calming Russian warmongering vis-à-vis Ukraine: 'Mister President, how many times have you negotiated with Putin and what have you achieved? Have you put an end to any of these actions? We don't negotiate with war criminals, we fight them. Would you have negotiated with Hitler, Stalin or Pol Pot?'[1]

No matter that Russia has the world's biggest nuclear arsenal, that it also has bacteriological and chemical weapons, that the Russian media kept saying that the tellingly named 'Satan II' hypersonic missiles could pulverise Paris in 200 seconds and London two seconds later; in the face of an aggressor, of the threat of nuclear blackmail brandished by 'a war criminal', of bloodthirsty despots, in short, in the face of the devil, war is just. For Prime Minister Morawiecki, this was a war of values waged in the name of freedom, democracy and the rule of law against tyranny. It was a conflict that had to be fought, even at the risk of starting a total war; negotiating with a tyrant was simply foolhardy.

Morawiecki's press conference took place thirty-nine days after Russia invaded Ukraine in what would be a watershed moment for Europe. Yes, there had been the war between Georgia and Russia in 2008, followed six years later by the occupation of Crimea and later by Russian attacks in the Donbas, but this time the conflict was of a different order. It shattered the peace taken for granted by the continent's countries and disproved Montesquieu's idea that trade smoothed over differences. Western Europe woke up to the fact that it was dependent on Russian gas. Since the Russian aggression on 24 February 2022, the two largest countries in Europe had been at war, and that war had already taken an immense toll. More than four million Ukrainians had fled into exile. The city of Mariupol had been under siege for weeks. The Russian forces were refusing, on various pretexts, to open humanitarian corridors. And on that 3 April, the world had just discovered the bodies of hundreds of Ukrainian civilians after Russian forces withdrew from Bucha, near Kyiv.

Morawiecki's belief, and the heated words he used, were no doubt rooted in the existential threat faced by

Poland in the twentieth century and by the emotion of the moment. War's relationship to peace is forged in the cauldron of history. And while French President Macron wanted to avoid 'humiliating' Russia, bearing in mind the disastrous consequences of the 1919 Treaty of Versailles and the German revanchism it engendered, the Polish Prime Minister was thinking not of the First, but of the Second World War. He feared those whom Raymond Aron called 'the merchants of sleep': those who had advocated a policy of appeasement vis-à-vis Hitler, notably British Prime Minister Neville Chamberlain, who, on his return from the Munich conference, told a jubilant crowd that he believed he had struck a 'peace for our time'—words he would forever regret. We all know what happened next.

But let's go back to those first weeks of the war in Ukraine. On 4 April Ukrainian President Volodymyr Zelensky went to Bucha and denounced 'war crimes' that would be recognised 'as genocide'.[2] Unlike Morawiecki, however, Zelensky had been quick to affirm his desire to negotiate: 'I'm ready for negotiations with [Putin] ... I think that without negotiations we cannot end this war.'[3] A few weeks later he explicitly stated on Ukrainian television: 'Discussions between Ukraine and Russia will definitely take place. I don't know in what format, with intermediaries or without them, in a wider circle, at the presidential level. There are things that we can only achieve at the negotiating table ... The war will be bloody, but it can only be ended once and for all through diplomacy.'[4]

The fortunes of war, shifts in the balance of power and on the battlefield, and political developments will prompt each party to change its position: if there is one thing we can be sure of, it is that war has its own unpredictable logic. At some point, unless the conflict descends into a deadly spiral, as it did during the First World War, or into a total war, as it did in the Second, the time will come to negotiate. On the basis of the balance of power on the ground, the belligerents will then discuss the price of peace, who controls what territory and their respective security imperatives.

The illusion of telling the devil ... to go to the devil

At that point, should we negotiate with the devil? With war criminals who have violated the most fundamental norms of humanity? In peace negotiations, it would be morally satisfying but delusional to tell the devil to go to the devil, because, as Paul Ricoeur writes, 'If politics were sent to the devil, reason itself would capsize'.[5] According to Clausewitz, violence is part of politics, and war the continuation of politics by other means.

And when British Prime Minister Winston Churchill said, 'If Hitler invaded hell I would make at least a favourable reference to the devil in the House of Commons',[6] he was implying that sometimes it is necessary to come to terms with the devil to save your country. A fierce anti-communist, Churchill thus justified his alliance with Stalin against Hitler, his reference to the devil indicating that the choice was not between good and evil, but between the lesser of two evils.

We must also ask ourselves if negotiating with war criminals—including the worst of them—might save lives. One example is the odious haggling in 1944 between Rudolf Katzner, a Jew from Transylvania, and Adolf Eichmann, the man behind the Final Solution. In exchange for the liberation of one million Jews, the Allies would deliver 10,000 trucks for Nazi Germany to use on the Eastern Front. Some 1,600 Jews doomed to certain death were taken on 'Freedom trains' to Switzerland as an 'advance payment' for a transaction that never took place. In another example, during the final weeks of the war the president of the Swedish Red Cross, Count Folke Bernadotte, negotiated with senior Nazi officials for the release from the concentration camps of thousands of Scandinavian prisoners who were repatriated to Europe in the 'White Buses' operation. More recently, was it right to negotiate—to take an extreme example— with the Lord's Resistance Army (LRA), a particularly bloodthirsty armed group that forcibly recruited thousands of children in northern Uganda only to send them to their deaths or use them as sex slaves? With very few exceptions, the answer is yes, of course. In this case, the Ugandan authorities dispatched successive mediators to negotiate with the LRA. The 2006–2008 negotiations, which had the backing of the Swiss government,[7] stabilised the region and enabled one million displaced people to return to their homes. The key point is not to choose whom you talk to, but rather to determine whether the negotiations will save lives, so as to prevent a greater evil.

'The enemy of mankind'

The tactic of conjuring the image of the devil is as old as humankind itself, but the representations continuously evolve in light of the needs and political equations of the time. In ancient Rome, Cicero argued that pirates were 'the enemy of mankind' (*hostis humani generis*), for the 'pirate is not included in the number of lawful enemies, but is the common enemy of all'.[8] For a powerful state to designate who is the evil incarnate is a formidable prerogative, tantamount to a licence to kill in the name of a greater good.

Etymologically, the devil defeats, disunites; hence, the imperative need to expel from humanity those who embody evil, literally to outlaw and prosecute them. Their expulsion from the human race requires the establishment of moral categories to identify those to be excluded, followed by the enactment of specific legislation and often the creation of a judicial bureaucracy with special courts entrusted to a caste of professionals. It is the job of exorcists to cast out demons. In the Middle Ages, for instance, the Inquisition was a specialised jurisdiction of the Catholic Church that authorised the use of torture to obtain confessions from heretics and witches before they were burned to death in a fire that was believed to purify their souls. What a sense of power, to have the sovereign right to decide on the nature of evil and how to eradicate it! And as centuries have passed, the moral categories of the incarnation of evil have evolved according to the political imperatives of those in power.

During the period covered in this book—from the fall of the Berlin Wall in 1989 to the present day—and in reaction to the atrocities committed in the former Yugoslavia and in Rwanda, the enemy of the human race initially took on the image of the war criminal and orchestrator of genocides, at least from the perspective of Western governments and subsequently the United Nations. Christian Chartier, spokesperson for the ICTY, was particularly optimistic when he said that such criminals would 'find the entire world one open-air prison' until they were apprehended, tried, sentenced and incarcerated. This is the creed that took hold in the post-Cold War era with the development of international criminal justice.

Interestingly, the same principle of universal jurisdiction that was applied to try pirates on the high seas has been used in the twentieth and twenty-first centuries to prosecute those whom we designate as the incarnation of absolute evil. In the face of 'the enemy of mankind', to use Cicero's formula, the law detached itself from its territorial anchorage and emancipated itself of the national sovereignty to which it was traditionally bound. Driven by the human rights community, liberal interventionism was expanded by reviving Immanuel Kant's longstanding dream of a cosmopolitan law able to restrain 'radical evil' and chain the devil in the irons of the law. The key moment in this process is the trial, where, at least judicially, the enigma of evil is resolved. German essayist Hannah Arendt perfectly captured that moment, describing how the public had expected a cloven-hoofed Lucifer to appear at the 1961 Jerusalem trial of Adolf Eichmann, not the bland—therefore all the more chilling—bureaucrat of the Final Solution.[9]

The devil's new clothes

After the attacks of 11 September 2001 in the United States, the devil was transformed into the figure of the terrorist. Human rights organisations and liberal interventionism no longer had the wind in their sails; instead 'security issues' gained the upper hand during the 'war on terror' waged by the neo-conservatives of the Bush administration. The result was formidable: a concept reminiscent of Cicero's pirates—'unlawful combatant'—was taken off the shelf and dusted off, paving the way for unprecedented means of surveillance and international coordination to be put in place. The United Nations, the United States, the European Union and many other countries sanctioned increasingly long lists of people, organisations and even governments suspected of terrorism or of collusion with terrorist organisations. In the US, the CIA obtained authorisation to set up, in 'friendly countries' in Asia, Europe and North Africa, a network of secret prisons for interrogating these 'unlawful combatants'. But this new global campaign had another unfortunate consequence: the restriction of civil liberties by authoritarian regimes, who took advantage of the 'war on terror' to do so in the name of national security.

To the question of the limits that 'civilisation' and 'democracy' must set in their fight 'against terror', the Bush administration gave the same answer as Saint-Just: no freedom for the enemies of freedom.

Thus, two decades ago, the American government proudly claimed that it did not negotiate with the Taliban; it would eradicate them.[10] How could America, the paradigm for democracy, talk to criminals whose obscurantism was as thick as their beards, who cut off people's hands and prevented girls from going to school? It would take a war, and tens of thousands of fatalities, before the American government would negotiate its pitiful retreat from Afghanistan with the Taliban 'terrorists' in Doha. So much for 'defending civilisation'.

Another example: the United Nations, the United States and the European Union currently consider

Hamas a terrorist organisation; therefore, they refuse to negotiate with it. Yet it was the Western governments themselves that encouraged the Palestinian Authority to organise elections in 2006 and to allow Hamas to field candidates. And although the European Union deemed those elections to be 'regular', it never recognised Hamas' victory in Gaza, so as not to legitimatise an organisation it had proscribed. In fact, EU and US diplomats are forbidden from talking to Hamas members, as are UN officials, yet it is an open secret that, barring a radical change in the political situation, peace cannot be achieved without Palestinian armed groups. The current state of affairs did not stop Israel from concluding truces with Hamas thanks to Egyptian mediation in 2008, 2010, 2014 and 2021.

When hubris fractures the rule of law

As hubris gripped the administration of George W. Bush in the early 2000s during its war of civilisations, the bulwark of the rule of law started to crack. How far should democracies go to eradicate the devil? To the point that they begin to resemble him? In his memo of 1 August 2002,[11] White House Assistant Attorney General Jay S. Bybee authorised the CIA to use up to ten forms of torture for thirty days to get senior Al-Qaeda leader Abu Zubaydah to talk. The memo contains a precise list of the ten forms of torture—reminiscent of the ten plagues of Egypt—including strangulation, where the interrogator seizes the detainee by the neck to bring him closer and speak eyeball to eyeball, a form of torture that Bybee coyly referred to as an 'attention grasp'; walling, which consists in throwing a person whose head or neck has been wrapped in a collar against a wall; confining the inmate in a box containing insects; and waterboarding, which simulates drowning by forcibly filling the inmate's lungs with water.

The Bush administration did all it could to stake out the moral high ground and explain that the defence of democracy required exceptional measures: the whole world watched what its only superpower was doing, took note and often followed suit. The 'war on terror' moved the goalposts in terms of what was acceptable. Mediation, previously lauded, was pushed aside in favour of military solutions that turned out to be so many dead ends.

How then to end wars? The logic of exclusion based on simplistic moral categories, disconnected from the social dynamics of societies in conflict, had the effect of preventing dialogue, making it impossible to find an alternative to warmongering. It is only when the illusion of military victory in these supposedly just wars is dispelled that mediation can regain its place, allowing for non-violent alternatives to ongoing conflicts.

Anti-terrorism transformed into an abstract ideology is blind to local realities and social dynamics. Moreover, all too often it reflects a lack of knowledge of the situation on the ground, tinged with arrogance, by attaching the term 'terrorist' to armed groups regardless of whether or not they represent a significant voice in their community, and blind to the reasons that they sometimes enjoy popular support. Mali is a vivid example of this pitfall: the categorisations of evil introduced by the 'war on terror' have radicalised the situation there and led to escalating violence, with military victory out of reach.

Writing about totalitarianism in the twentieth century, Hannah Arendt defines ideology as an idea that dispenses with the usual function of thought to obey only its own logic and descend into madness, throwing off everything that might temper, limit or contradict it—to the point where the human mind is confined by what she calls the 'straitjacket of logic'.[12] There is, of course, no comparison between the outbreaks of totalitarianism that have caused tens of millions of deaths and the ideology of the 'war on terror', but the latter has also imprisoned itself in the straitjacket of its own logic.

3

FROM MORALITY TO HUBRIS

It was Herodotus who wrote that 'it is the gods' custom to bring low all things of surpassing greatness'.[1] In Greek mythology, there was no greater sin than pride, hubris—the belief that you could bend reality to your will. The hubris of the post-Cold War years of Pax Americana consisted in believing that evil could be eliminated, or at least controlled. That period may seem like a distant memory now, so full of illusions and alien to the world of today, but we continue to be governed by the rules that were established at the time and have been extended to today's conflicts, including Ukraine, but also twisted. International criminal justice, initially conceived as a contribution 'to the restoration and maintenance of peace',[2] has become a weapon of war, reshaping the space for mediation.

Thirty years ago, the vocabulary of politics was awash with morality. Religious terms—reconciliation, forgiveness, even the concept of international criminal justice—were part of the new mantra. The state, 'the coldest of all cold monsters', for which guile and reason of state had appeared to be the order of the day, suddenly seemed to come down on the side of Nelson Mandela rather than the icy realism of former US Secretary of State Henry Kissinger. In the zeitgeist prevailing after the fall of the Berlin Wall in 1989, politicians and the media spoke about the need for a 'peace dividend' in a world that was finally reconciled. When the Iron Curtain was brought down and defence budgets plummeted, we experienced a time of optimism and even of mad utopianism: the world would be rid of war, history having reached its final destination—liberal democracy. A bestseller at the time proclaimed 'the end of history'.[3] Encouraged by the world's surviving superpower, the UN adopted policies of peace and collective security in 'the new international order'.

What sparked this outbreak of morality in international politics? Admittedly, politics has always clothed itself in the discourse of virtue. Ronald Reagan, for example, called the Soviet Union the 'evil empire' while depicting his country as the embodiment of good; however, in the 1990s, morality, which defines the boundaries between good and evil, gained traction in international affairs in a situation of unprecedented hegemony by the world's remaining superpower, the United States. With the UN as its frontman, the US helped forge norms in the name of this new order, without renouncing the use of force and, cloaked in the legitimacy of the UN, it was able to spearhead the Gulf War in 1991 to restore the independence of Kuwait; it intervened militarily, again under a UN mandate, in Somalia in 1992; and subsequently launched military–humanitarian operations in Haiti, Rwanda, the former Yugoslavia, the Democratic Republic of the Congo and elsewhere.

At the same time, mediation became a major ideological marker of the values vaunted by the new international order: liberalism was the ultimate goal for societies whose transition to peace and democracy was being negotiated. Mediation was thus part of the broader vision of peace set out, for example, by UN Secretary-General Boutros Boutros-Ghali in 1992 in *An Agenda for Peace*, with mediators playing a central role in preventing disputes, drawing up and implementing peace agreements, and even addressing 'the deepest causes of conflict: economic despair, social injustice and political oppression'.[4]

In dozens of countries emerging from conflict, from Nepal to El Salvador, Pax Americana left its mark on conflict settlements. The 1995 Dayton Accords, which brought a temporary halt to the hostilities in the former Yugoslavia, are one example. From this perspective, the end of an armed confrontation was seen as a 'democratic window of opportunity' to be seized. Guided by the iconic figure of Nelson Mandela, its newly elected head of state, post-apartheid South Africa led the way in achieving a peaceful transition. Peace was redefined: it now came with an ideological toolkit comprising democracy, good governance, the fight against impunity, the restoration or establishment of the rule of law, human rights, anti-corruption action, transparency, economic development, open markets and neo-liberal globalisation. We will see later that reality fell far short of that ambitious goal, but it all sure sounded good at the time.

Mediation grew spectacularly in the 1980s and 1990s, settling more conflicts in those twenty years alone than during the previous half-century. The predominant vision of peace was technocratic but also militarised, grounded in the concept of an all-powerful UN acting simultaneously as global mediator, super-cop, justice of the peace and architect of the reconstruction of post-conflict societies. In 1992, the UN also published *The Handbook on the Peaceful Settlement of Disputes between States*, which focused on inter-state mediation. As David Harland of the Centre for Humanitarian Dialogue aptly phrased it, those were 'the glorious years'[5] of mediation, with peace being agreed by Iran and Iraq in 1988, the tripartite agreement leading to Namibia's independence that same year, and the conclusion of peace agreements in Lebanon (Ta'if, 1989), Nicaragua (Tela, 1989), Cambodia (Paris, 1991), El Salvador (Chapultepec, 1992), Croatia (Erdut, 1995) and Guatemala (Guatemala City, 1995). In 1992, Sant'Egidio, a religious community on the outskirts of Rome, managed to bring an end to the terrible civil war

ravaging Mozambique—the first time a private organisation led a peace process, hitherto the domain of the UN
and states.

Human rights morality attacks mediation

But two major events in the early 1990s forced the UN
fundamentally to rethink the place of mediation. What
role should mediators play in the face of the horrific
events in Bosnia-Herzegovina (1992–1995) and Rwanda
(1994)? What does the very concept of the mediator's
neutrality mean when confronted by genocide or crimes
against humanity?

Neutrality, it must be remembered, implies drawing a
moral equivalence between the belligerents, regardless of
the crimes that one or the other may have committed.
We will see in the second part of this book that the
ICRC was the first to come up against this problem,
during the Second World War; then how the UN would
in turn position itself vis-à-vis the war crimes committed
in the former Yugoslavia and later in Syria. The issues
raised by having mediators find a middle ground with
the perpetrators of mass violence were now squarely on
the table.

In parallel to the questions being asked about the
moral limits of mediation, and in reaction to the crimes
committed in the Balkans and in Rwanda, steps were
taken to develop the international criminal justice sys-

tem. This also transformed the space for mediation. The backers of the international criminal tribunals for the former Yugoslavia and Rwanda, and in 2002 of the International Criminal Court, established a new principle: war criminals should be excluded from peace processes. From that point on, the tension between the search for peace and the demand for justice has been palpable, from the former Yugoslavia to Liberia, in Sudan, the Central African Republic, Libya and elsewhere. And it persists to the present day, even though Articles 16 and 53 of the Rome Statute of the International Criminal Court[6] reflect the attempt, in vain, to introduce a measure of flexibility and despite endeavours to correctly sequence transitional or post-conflict justice mechanisms.

The debate on 'peace versus justice' has been marked from the outset by two vigorously opposed points of view.[7] In an article for *Human Rights Quarterly*, Richard Goldstone, the Chief Prosecutor of the ICTY, writes: 'A peace masterminded by and in order to accommodate the concerns of vicious war criminals defiant of all the fundamental international law prescriptions or norms is [not an] effective or enduring peace.'[8] That view drew a scathing response from one of the principal advisers to the mediators at the International Conference on the Former Yugoslavia, an anonymous 'Mr X': 'The quest for justice for yesterday's victims ... should not be pursued in such a manner that it makes today's living the dead of tomorrow. That, for the human rights community, is one of the lessons of the former Yugoslavia. Thousands of people are dead who should have been alive—because moralists were in quest of the perfect peace. Unfortunately, a perfect peace can rarely be attained in the aftermath of a bloody conflict. The pursuit of criminals is one thing; making peace is another.'[9]

The two men disagreed because they had different definitions of peace. For Mr X, peace is restored at the end of hostilities. It is a negative peace as opposed to the positive peace to which Goldstone aspired, a peace that would fit within the liberal-peace paradigm, a reconciled society its ultimate goal. Ironically, Goldstone, despite his strong words, prosecuted only small fry. Serbian President Slobodan Milosevic, who signed the Dayton Agreement in 1995, was not indicted until much later, during the conflict in Kosovo. In other words, Milosevic was politically useful until the end the war in Bosnia-Herzegovina but had become a source of instability in the conflict in Kosovo. His indictment in 1999 by the ICTY, including for incidents dating back to the wars in Croatia in 1991 and Bosnia in 1992, was ultimately based more on political than legal considerations.

I was delighted by that indictment. I had seen the ravages wrought by 'ethnic cleansing' in Bosnia and had been among the first to arrive at the scene of the Račak massacre in Kosovo, which triggered Milosevic's indictment, the first by an international court. After the massacres in Bosnia, the camps, the policies of forced displacement, the thought that the national leader who had set the Balkans ablaze would be held to account was more than a little alluring. I saw the advantages of delegitimising and prosecuting him without, however, exonerating the other perpetrators of war crimes, regardless of the camp to which they belonged. Since then, and despite the conviction that we must fight impunity, I have become increasingly sceptical about the overtly political and selective ends to which international justice is used.

One of the most radical examples of this new judicial diplomacy is arguably the wilful decision of David Crane, an American lawyer who was the Chief Prosecutor of the Special Court for Sierra Leone, to torpedo the UN-organised peace conference. In June 2003, he indicted Liberian President Charles Taylor, justifying his decision as follows: 'I wanted to show West Africans that no one is above the law, that the rule of law is more powerful than the rule of guns, that with the stroke of a pen a warlord can be discredited in the eyes of his peers. My intention was not to have Charles Taylor arrested. I wanted to remove him from the peace process.'[10] This particularly striking example shows an American prosecutor, whose country was at the time waging a veritable crusade against the International Criminal Court,[11] arrogating to himself the right to decide who is or is not qualified to participate in a UN peace conference. All this, on the staggering pretext of teaching Africans a lesson in democracy and the rule of law—at a time when four African heads of state were participating in the peace conference, which was itself hosted by Ghana, UN Secretary-General Kofi Annan's home country. Crane's vision of the law as all powerful reflected both the concept of holy war and a worrisome judicial neo-imperialism capable of supplanting a planned process of mediation.

International justice versus the search for peace?

Crane was drunk on power, but politicians and even the militants of various causes—European governments, African heads of state, Palestinian activists, for once united—soon grasped the political usefulness of international criminal justice. They gave short shrift to the Kantian outlook advocated by Crane but saw clearly how they could exploit international criminal justice for their own ends, to introduce their own narrative in the public sphere—a process for which the Americans coined the term 'lawfare'. The aim was not so much to prosecute war crimes (that was the job of the court) but to point a finger at the culprit in the court of public opinion, to 'weaponise' international justice, transforming it into a weapon of war that would embed its version of the truth in the public mind by filing charges and issuing indictments. The reversal could not have been more complete: international criminal justice, initially conceived as a contribution 'to the restoration and maintenance of peace',[12] was being used to various political ends, whether tactically to 'extract' troublesome leaders (such as Bosnian Serb leaders Radovan Karadzic and Ratko Mladic in 1995) from peace talks and facilitate an agreement (Dayton), to delegitimise one of the parties, or to legitimise military intervention.

The West thus used the International Criminal Court to delegitimise the erratic Libyan dictator Muammar Gaddafi, when NATO was preparing to intervene militarily in the country. On 26 February 2011, the UN Security Council asked the Court to investigate the international crimes committed in Libya. Six days later, Court Prosecutor Luis Moreno Ocampo announced that an investigation had been opened; Gaddafi was indicted in a matter of weeks, justifying NATO's military intervention. The aspiration of human rights organisations for international justice with no political interference gave way to increasingly blatant exploitation.

This departure from the Court's original purpose persists. The Court's current activism in Ukraine is emblematic of this development, which constrains the space for mediation. While it took years for the Court to act in respect of Afghanistan, Israel-Palestine and elsewhere, Prosecutor Karim Khan has been as quick to intervene in Ukraine as his predecessor was in Libya. Only four days after the Russian invasion, Khan declared his intention to launch a war-crimes investigation. Forty-eight hours later, thirty-nine countries—almost all of them

NATO members or militarily allied with the US[13]—
asked the Court to launch an inquiry and decided to
finance its work in Ukraine,[14] a country that has yet to
ratify the Rome Statute (!) but simply recognised the
Court's jurisdiction after the Russian attacks in Crimea
and the Donbas in 2014. The Court's decision is all the
more surprising in that, under Article 17 of the Rome
Statute, cases are admissible on a subsidiary basis only if
'the State is unwilling or unable' to prosecute those bearing the greatest responsibility for international crimes.
Ukraine, it must be remembered, moved very quickly to
sentence Russian soldiers charged with war crimes, and
its judicial system remains especially active.

Western public opinion, understandably outraged at
the Russian aggression and destruction of cities and
lives, just as understandably felt the need to send a message of solidarity to a country under attack; however, the
fact remains that the International Criminal Court
seems to have become the legal arm enabling NATO to
delegitimise Russian power, abetted by President Biden
using the term 'genocide'[15] to describe the crimes committed by the Russian army.[16] In the face of the Court's
activism, former Russian President Dmitry Medvedev,
currently the Deputy Chairman of Russia's Security
Council, blew up. Resorting to blackmail, he brandished
the threat of nuclear weapons (!) if the Court pursued its
work, betraying his vision of a world reduced to a confrontation between great powers, where nothing can

limit the use of the most brutal force: 'The idea of punishing the country that has the largest nuclear arsenal is absurd in itself. And it potentially threatens the existence of mankind.'[17]

Who could have imagined that international criminal justice, which was supposed to be a contribution 'to the restoration and maintenance of peace', would one day help escalate a conflict to the point of a threatened thermonuclear holocaust?

4

TO NEGOTIATE OR NOT TO NEGOTIATE?

As we saw in the previous chapter, international criminal justice had become caught up in conflict dynamics; however, the 'war on terror' would have an even more radical impact on peace processes. It stopped mediators from having any contact with organisations labelled 'terrorist', and thereby risked further radicalising armed groups.

Seventeen days after the attacks of 11 September 2001 on the twin towers in New York and the Pentagon, the UN Security Council unanimously adopted resolution 1373, which, together with resolution 1267 (1999), adopted after the attacks on the American embassies in Dar es Salaam and Nairobi, would form the core of the international anti-terrorist system subsequently put in place. President Bush's message was crystal clear: 'Every nation in every region now has a decision to make: Either you are with us or you are with the terrorists.'[1] According to him, the ultimate goal of this crusade of 'civilisation against terror' was to end tyranny in our world.[2] The EU immediately followed suit and banned certain individuals and organisations. This time around, it wasn't the human rights movement that wanted to limit mediation with war criminals, but the neo-conservatives holding sway in the Bush administration, whose 'just war' was intended to hunt down and, if possible, eradicate 'the terrorists'. Drawing on the tropes of American Westerns, they printed posters putting a price on the heads of Osama bin Laden and other outlaws.

This was hardly the first time armed groups had been banned, but the fact that the ban was worldwide was unprecedented, as were the means deployed internationally to implement it. The two Security Council resolutions were adopted under Chapter VII of the UN Charter, the only chapter that authorises the use of force to uphold international peace and security. Resolution 1373 requires Member States not only to prevent and suppress terrorist acts, but also to:

> prohibit their nationals or any persons and entities within their territories from making any funds, financial assets or economic resources or financial or other related services available, directly or indirectly, for the benefit of persons who commit or attempt to commit or facilitate or participate in the commission of terrorist acts, of entities owned or controlled, directly or indirectly, by such persons and of persons and entities acting on behalf of or at the direction of such persons.[3]

Never before had UN Member States been required to implement a resolution that set no deadline or specific conditions. Nor did the resolution define 'terrorism', allowing governments to call any organisations they deemed hostile or dangerous 'terrorist'. This gave authoritarian governments, as in Uganda, the perfect pretext for legitimising policies of arbitrary repression in the name of national security. A black-and-white view of conflicts took hold, in which no one but the 'terrorists' was responsible for the violence, and which ignored the complex nature of conflicts and undermined more effective peace-building strategies.

The American administration also changed its strategy on mediation: hitherto heralded as the expression of the new post-Cold War international order, mediation was now perceived as an admission of weakness. After the UN legitimised the 'war on terror', the Bush administration started to see mediation as a check on the policy of regime change and the export of democracy, if necessary by force. The 2003 invasion of Iraq by the US, without a UN mandate, testifies to that radical change in course. The Americans directed their entire security apparatus at the military defeat of Saddam Hussein and 'the terrorists'—despite the fact that the two weren't really connected—and swept the rest of the world along with them.

If you exclude terrorists, how then do you talk to them?

The establishment of lists of terrorist organisations was nonetheless problematic, especially since some of the organisations concerned had achieved power in undisputed elections (e.g. Hamas and Hezbollah, which represented part of the electorate). Hence the hesitation of Western governments: what should take precedence, the 'anti-terrorist' fight or the election results? The United Nations, the European Union, the United States, the United Kingdom—their lists were not always the same. For example, while the armed wing of Hamas appeared on the initial 2001 list of the United States, it was only under pressure from London and Washington that the European Union followed suit in 2003, France and Belgium having opposed such a move until then, with a view to possible peace negotiations.[4] On the other hand, only the military arm of Hezbollah was labelled terrorist: according to the European Union, Lebanon had to be supported 'with all the political parties present'. Most surprisingly, the United States listed the Taliban leaders, but not the organisation itself, as if it were making allowances for the possibility of a future peace agreement as early as 2001.

Organisations are easily added to such lists; it is much more complicated to remove them. For the European Union list of terrorist organisations, all twenty-seven Member States have to agree before an armed group can be removed. It took five years (!) after the conclusion of the peace agreement between the Colombian government and the Revolutionary Armed Forces of Colombia (FARC) for the latter to no longer appear on American lists of 'terrorist organisations'.[5]

A chilling effect on official mediation

During the 1990s, official mediation in armed conflicts conducted by the UN and by states (such as the US, Norway and Switzerland) expanded impressively. The trend was reversed with the 'war on terror'[6]—understandably so: in 1989, there were no armed conflicts in which one party was officially labelled 'terrorist' by the UN, while half of today's conflicts involve 'terrorist organisations',[7] often radical Islamist groups that have been proscribed.

Many of those conflicts are beyond the reach of a military solution, yet governments have continued to chant the mantra, 'We will never negotiate with terrorists', limiting their options for a resolution and thus prolonging the conflict and its tragic consequences—but what does that matter? The war on terror outweighs all other considerations.

Also, resolution 1373 effectively puts mediators at risk of prosecution if they even so much as offer 'the terrorists' a coffee, or encourage them to join talks, or pay the travel costs of members of an armed group to facilitate dialogue. Suffice it for the armed group to be on the list published by the US Office of Foreign Assets Control (OFAC). This is the outcome of the United States Supreme Court decision in *Holder v. Humanitarian Law Project* (2010), in which the Supreme Court asserted that anyone—even non-Americans or non-residents of the United States—who provided training, advocacy or expert advice or assistance to 'a terrorist organization' was committing an illegal act and would be prosecuted if they received US funds.

The NGO Norwegian People's Aid (NPA) had to pay a more than US$2 million fine for having organized a seminar on democracy in Gaza for young people aged fifteen to twenty-eight; the participants included members of Hamas, the Popular Front for the Liberation of Palestine (PFLP) and the Democratic Front for the Liberation of Palestine (DFLP).[8] The NPA had previously received US funding for emergency aid to South Sudan, funding that had nothing to do with the seminar in Gaza, but the fact that the NPA had benefited from American money was deemed enough to prosecute them. True, the case involved a humanitarian organisation as opposed to a mediator, but it fostered an atmosphere of intimidation and self-censorship that also affected the mediation community.

A striking example of this self-imposed diplomatic paralysis was the experience of mediator Alvaro de Soto, the UN Secretary-General's Special Coordinator for the Middle East Peace Process until his resignation in May 2007. Owing to American pressure, de Soto was prohibited from talking to the Syrian government or senior Hamas officials. Yet the latter had been voted into office in Gaza in elections organised at the behest of the same Western governments that considered Hamas, which controls some two million Palestinians, a 'terrorist' organisation. This makes little sense—even the Israeli authorities negotiate truces and prisoner swaps through Egypt with Hamas. In his confidential fifty-three-page report, which was leaked to the media, de Soto expressed frustration with his superiors at the United Nations, who were eager to win the support of the American administration at all costs: 'At best I have been the UN special coordinator for the Middle East peace process in name only, and since the election of Hamas, I have been the secretary-general's personal representative to the Palestinian Authority for about 10 minutes in two phone calls and one handshake.'[9] De Soto tendered his resignation when UN Secretary-General Ban Ki-moon informed him that any future meetings with the Prime Minister of the Palestinian Authority would hinge on the assessment of his policy made by the UN Secretariat, whose chief concern was not to antagonise the United States. What can mediators do if they can't meet with the parties?

Enter the NGOs able to talk unofficially with 'terrorists'

Time and again, government anti-terrorist action came up against the same problem: how could it exclude the 'terrorists' and at the same time leave the door open to dialogue with them? Indeed, the international hunt for and eradication of 'terrorist organisations' launched in 2001 did not have the anticipated results in Afghanistan,

Pakistan, Mali, Syria, Iraq, Somalia, Colombia, Palestine and elsewhere. In a surprising turn of events, such dialogue returned to the international stage by another door: private mediation organisations, which, while funded for the most part by European governments, found a niche in the contradiction facing these same governments and others. Since it was no longer possible for either the United Nations or the states to talk with organisations labelled 'terrorist', informal players discreetly entered the scene.

It was around this time that the largest private mediation organisations were established: the Centre for Humanitarian Dialogue, founded in 1999 in Geneva, is the successor of the Centre Henry Dunant, which was part of the Red Cross Movement. In 2000, the Crisis Management Initiative was established in Helsinki by former Finnish President Martti Ahtisaari, winner of the 2008 Nobel Peace Prize 'for his important efforts, on several continents ... to resolve international conflicts',[10] particularly in Namibia, Indonesia (Aceh) and Kosovo. In the following years, other mediation NGOs were established and existing NGOs became involved in the field of mediation: the Carter Center in the US; Berghof Foundation in Germany; Conciliation Resources and Inter Mediate in Great Britain; Swisspeace in Switzerland; the African Centre for the Constructive Resolution of Disputes (ACCORD) in South Africa; the Institute for Economics and Peace in Brussels; and others.

It was thanks to mediation NGOs like these that talks got under way with ETA in the Basque Country, with the FARC in Colombia, with Hamas and the PFLP in Palestine, with the armed wing of Lebanon's Hezbollah, the Afghan Taliban, the Kurdish PKK and dozens of other armed groups in Syria, along with jihadist groups in Mali and the rest of the Sahel (see Chapter 10). Many governments and regional organisations, such as the African or European Union, quickly realised the advantages of 'outsourcing' negotiations, at least in the initial phase of peace processes. Governments see in such organisations—which can act swiftly and discreetly, and which represent only themselves—a way of squaring the circle, their discreet activities all the easier to deny in that they are not accountable to public opinion, but only to their donors, whether governments or regional organisations such as the European or African Union. Although this has sometimes earned them the exaggerated epithet of 'cowboys',[11] private mediation organisations lay the groundwork, establish contact with armed groups, explore different options, identify the key players and test possible solutions, allowing states to limit the risks of immediately profiling themselves as a mediating party. If massacres occur while mediation is taking place, or if the negotiations fail, it becomes difficult for a mediating state to justify its role to its citizens. That attitude may be hypocritical, but at least it's pragmatic. And, as Berghof Foundation senior advisor Véronique

Dudouet points out,[12] what choice do the states have? Peace agreements have little chance of success if they exclude armed groups with a strong predilection for causing trouble and which sometimes represent a substantial part of the population. How could the Israeli–Palestinian conflict be resolved without the agreement of Palestinian armed groups?

Dialogue can also save lives in humanitarian negotiations by, for instance, arranging for food to be brought to populations living in besieged cities. Dialogue also helps remove the psychological barrier of 'them or us' binary survival logic. This was the experience of Jonathan Powell, then Chief of Staff to British Prime Minister Tony Blair, in the Northern Ireland conflict: Powell recognised that if the British government had been less intransigent about refusing to talk with the IRA over the years, a peace agreement could have been concluded earlier and lives could have been saved. Since then, Powell has championed the 'talk to terrorists' approach in his book *Talking to Terrorists*,[13] which contains an endless list of governments that have said they would never negotiate with terrorists but then did.

However, let me be clear: not all armed groups are willing to talk. Some, such as the Shining Path in Peru, never are. Nor has Islamic State ever shown an interest in dialogue.

Whatever the virtues of mediation NGOs, they are limited by their very nature. Except in a very few cases, they do not enjoy sufficient legitimacy to conclude peace agreements and, although they claim to be independent, they remain essentially dependent for their financing on the public purse of European countries.

There is no getting around the essential fact: the rigidity of the anti-terrorist system put in place in 2001 was tremendously counterproductive. The emergence of private diplomacy, with all its limits, was a tacit admission of this failure that would take time to rectify. In the meantime, many wars and lives were lost.

5

THE END OF PAX AMERICANA

As we have seen, for two glorious decades American hegemony fostered an environment conducive to United Nations mediation and the conclusion of peace agreements. That changed when the 'war on terror' was launched after 11 September 2001, soft power giving way to military interventions in Iraq, Afghanistan and Libya, and to regime change. This was followed by a third phase: the erosion of American power and the emergence of a new international equation, with Russia and the United States at loggerheads while China and other regional powers grew in strength. In this multipolar world, in which states have enough power to counter one country's domination of the international system, the rules of war-time engagement are being called into question, thus limiting the ability of mediators to act. The tectonic plates of international politics are shifting, as most recently seen with Russian revanchism bolstered by Washington's deregulation of the use of force against a backdrop of Western decline and the rise of China and regional powers.

The natural mediator of the 1990s par excellence, the United Nations is largely dependent on a unified Security Council. The Security Council is increasingly riven by division unwittingly initiated by the United States, which marginalised the UN and disregarded international law in a moment of ideological hubris after the Cold War, thus sparking a chain reaction.

The military intervention in Iraq, launched in the face of Security Council opposition and predicated on a lie (the existence of weapons of mass destruction), sent a clear signal: if the United States could shrug at the law and invade a country that had neither pro-voked it nor killed one of its citizens, why should other powers that were less attentive to human rights and respect for the law of war not also do as they please? In an abysmal slip that sounded like an unconscious admission of guilt, former US President George W. Bush, speaking about Ukraine in early 2022, referred to 'the brutal and unjustified invasion ... of Iraq'. What a change from his years in power, when the neo-con-servatives in the White House were under the illusion that America could reshape the Middle East and export 'democracy' by might. After all, according to the macho formula[1] in vogue across the Atlantic, don't Americans come from Mars and the fainthearted Europeans from Venus?

In retrospect, it was the 1999 NATO intervention in Kosovo that served as the testing ground for the deregulated use of force. NATO acted without Security Council backing, in the name of humanitarian necessity: a third of the Albanian population had been driven out of Kosovo and, absent outside intervention, disaster loomed. It was, in the words of Gilad Ben-Nun, Professor of Global Studies at Leipzig University, 'a *felix culpa* [mistake with happy consequences] crucial for the Balkans, but which will have disastrous consequences for international security'.[2] By first bypassing the United Nations and then wresting a resolution from the Security Council to legitimise military action after the fact, NATO and its 1999 military victory in Kosovo paved the way for the invasion of Iraq in 2003. Melbourne University Professor of Law Anne Orford underscored the depth of American hubris: 'Kosovo, and later Iraq, represented a possible dystopian future in which powerful states or coalitions of willing states marginalized the United Nations and set themselves up as representatives of humanity.'[3]

United States policy thus became a source of global political and diplomatic tension. One of the first leaders to state his opposition to the new policy was Vladimir Putin, who, in a speech at the 2007 Munich Security Conference, denounced US hubris, deeming the unipolar model and domination of the international system by the American superpower alone as 'not only unacceptable but also impossible'.[4] An autocrat himself, Putin nonetheless and ironically gave the United States a moral lesson, pointing out the dangers of hubris in a unipolar world where:

> there is one master, one sovereign. And at the end of the day this is pernicious not only for all those within this system, but also for the sovereign itself because it destroys itself from within. And this certainly has nothing in common with democracy. Because, as you know, democracy is the power of the majority in light of the interests and opinions of the minority.

In view of the Russian invasion of Ukraine, Putin might be well-advised to apply what he said in 2007 to himself, but in 2008, he felt free to attack Georgia, which had shaken off the Russian yoke. As Barack Obama observed in retrospective comments on that period, Putin was emboldened by the waning power of an America caught between an economic crisis and the calamitous management of Hurricane Katrina:

> The international order (the Pax Americana) was still in place in the spring of 2009. But faith in American leadership had been shaken ... We have beckoned the world to follow us into a paradisiacal land of free markets, global supply chains, internet connections, easy credit and democratic governance. And for the moment, at least, it felt to them like they might have followed us over a cliff.[5]

The turning point—Libya

The turning point came in March 2011, when NATO intervened in Libya. The United States and the Arab League convinced Russian President Dmitry Medvedev (Putin was then Prime Minister) and China not to oppose Security Council resolution 1973 on 'the responsibility to protect', which was used to justify NATO's intervention. But then the military–humanitarian operation changed. For NATO, the point was no longer to protect the people living under the Gaddafi regime— they were no longer threatened—but to seize the opportunity to overthrow it. Robert Gates, then US Secretary of Defense, warned the West that this abuse of power was a huge mistake: 'The Russians felt they had been played for suckers on Libya. They felt there had been a bait and switch. I said at the time we would pay hell for ever getting them to cooperate in the future.'[6]

In fact, it was the Syrian population that would 'pay hell'. From that point on, the Russian government would oppose the principle of 'the responsibility to protect', arguing that it was no more than a pretext for Western interventionism, just like human rights. When, in October 2011, Bashar al-Assad's regime ordered a ruthless campaign of repression and the fighting in the country turned bloody, Russian Ambassador Vitaly Churkin invoked the precedent of Libya to justify the Russian and Chinese veto:

> The situation in Syria cannot be considered in the Council separately from the Libyan experience. The international community is alarmed by statements that compliance with Security Council resolutions on Libya in the NATO interpretation is a model for the future actions of NATO in implementing the responsibility to protect.[7]

Ever since, Russia has objected to any resolution submitted by NATO's countries aimed at curbing Assad, and as a result countless Syrians have been killed, tortured, displaced and starved. All the parties to the Syrian conflict have committed war crimes but the Syrian army and its cronies have been no less savage. The Russian army, in particular, has replicated outside its own territory the brutal 'steamroller' strategy it got away with in Chechnya in the 1990s, pounding cities until there was nothing left standing and with no regard for civilian populations, violating the law of armed conflict[8] and international human rights law, which all the States are bound to respect. The law of armed conflict (also called international humanitarian law or IHL) protects people who do not take part in the fighting and imposes limits on the means and methods of warfare. No longer was it only the likes of al-Qaeda or the Islamic State who were committing atrocities, it was now also the United States, lifting all restraints by deregulating the use of force in Iraq and Afghanistan; and the Russian army, who then notched up that approach in Syria. Russia had few qualms when its air force carpet-bombed Syrian cities held by rebels or, in the spring of 2022, Mariupol in Ukraine.

The constraints of counterterrorism after 11 September 2001 and the divisions within the UN Security Council have contributed to further reducing the space for official mediation as the period of American hegemony draws to a close.

Taking stock of Pax Americana

Dozens of countries in Africa, Latin America, Asia and Europe have experienced transition under the spreading branches of ideology and instruments of liberal peace, but only rarely have those branches borne fruit in terms of democracy, human rights and development. Peace agreements have not had the anticipated results: of thirty-three such agreements concluded between 1989 and 2012, twenty-seven use the words 'democracy' and 'elections'.[9] A comparison of several peace agreements reveals striking similarities, as if, under the impulse of the United Nations, concepts of 'democracy' had been mechanically inserted, establishing a state bureaucracy intended to create the rule of law, an independent judiciary, and economic development. A vertical and top-down peace like this reflects the naiveté of international organisations in the face of extraordinarily fragile societies trying to extricate themselves from years of conflict.

Sadly, results of the agreements fall short of expectations, and there are a number of reasons why mediation has had such mediocre results.

In dozens of countries the old elites have either re-emerged or agreed to share power with the new; democracy, the rule of law and economic development have failed to materialise. In Bosnia-Herzegovina, despite massive investment by Western governments and the international community (which have gone so far as to design the new national flag), the state is hamstrung by nationalist sentiment and has become dysfunctional. The incredibly ambitious 2006 Darfur peace agreement[10] provided for the distribution of wealth, power sharing, and the establishment of justice and reparation processes. Once again, however, the political differences between the parties proved to be too deeply ingrained. Egged on by the UN Security Council, the mediators involved in the negotiations 'lost sight of the distinction between getting the parties to sign an agreement and obtaining their real commitment to its terms and implementation'.[11] In a very ethnocentric vision, mediators have succumbed to the fetishism of the piece of paper, which supposedly symbolises the peace agreement and the road to national reconciliation. They have been too quick to ignore the internal dynamics of societies.

According to the Freedom House State of Democracy Index and the Transparency International Corruption Index, countries that have been major recipients of international aid in support of a peace process (Burundi, Cambodia, the Central African Republic, Côte d'Ivoire, Iraq, Nepal, Rwanda, South Sudan and many others) are characterised by a form of internal functioning that is neither free (absence or restriction of civil and political rights) nor transparent. In a particularly candid document,[12] British Foreign Office experts observe that many peace agreements break down either because one party believes that the balance of power has shifted in its favour and that the previously signed agreement is null and void, or because local elites are strong enough to resist the reforms agreed. In academic circles, Professors Roger McGinty, Roland Paris and Oliver Richmond,[13] among others, have been scathing about 'Ikea Peace' and its neo-colonial overtones, criticising it as a form of peace that is exported, assembled and disassembled, its constituent elements cut and pasted, its toolbox replicated from one country to another, most often ignoring local conditions and the needs of the population, and proving ultimately to be both costly and ineffective.

In 2009, UN Secretary-General Ban Ki-moon commissioned a report on enhancing mediation and its support activities. In it, the optimism of Boutros Boutros-Ghali's 1992 report gives way to a lucid analysis of the many challenges facing UN mediation, conceding even that 'too often in the past, mediators have been dispatched without the full benefit of specialized training and background information, giving United Nations efforts an ad hoc quality too dependent on trial and error';[14] further, it addresses the tension between the pursuit of peace and justice, discusses the issue of inclusivity and the 'saboteurs' of peace processes, and recognises the useful role of private organisations in the mediation of armed conflicts.

Since the report was published, the United Nations has become even more marginalised as a result of an increasingly divided international community. The wars in Iraq, Syria, Ukraine and elsewhere are evidence of this. Gone are the days when an American undersecretary of state could summon heads of state to a military base in Ohio and lock them up together until they had hammered out a solution to the war in the Balkans—the Dayton Agreement. Today, without indulging in romanticism and without being overly pragmatic, effective mediation must pay closer attention to the social, political and cultural dynamics specific to each conflict, a reconfiguration, or perhaps a correction, reflecting the re-emergence of a multipolar world, the deregulation of the use of force and the erosion of international norms. Mediators have always been relatively powerless but, at least at certain times— notably in the immediate post-Cold War period—they could count on a broadly supportive political environment and a certain amount of swagger; now, however, they are called upon to show some humility, their room for manoeuvre curtailed, yet with moral challenges just

as daunting. How can they ride the wave without sink-
ing on the shoals of complicity? This is the subject of
the second part of this book.

PART TWO

IN SEARCH OF THE LESSER EVIL

6

FROM COMPROMISE TO COMPLICITY?

In the first part of this book, I described how the tension between excluding and including 'enemies of human-kind' has played out since the end of the Cold War and how the space for mediation has been transformed by the development of international criminal justice during times of war and by the 'war on terror'. The terms of the discussion having thus been set, I will now descend from the exalted spheres of diplomacy and law to the nitty gritty of mediation in several borderline situations, such as the process of human selection I mentioned in the introduction. My purpose is not to cast a moralising eye on past events, but rather to outline a critical approach based on real experience, as an aid to action and a means of moving forward in a grey zone where moral safe-guards are easily blurred.

Surgeons obey their Hippocratic Oath when they operate; likewise, mediators must also heed a moral imperative: to avoid adding to the suffering or the death toll. Just as the Greek word *phármakon*—medicine—can also mean poison, the mediator's action might veer from striking a necessary compromise with the perpetrators of war crimes to being complicit with them. Philosopher Paul Ricoeur explains the difference: in a compromise, 'everyone remains true to their position'; complicity involves 'a vicious combination of plans and basic principles' that betrays the objective of the mission.[1]

'There is a hazy but very real line beyond which aid for the victims clearly becomes support for the executioners,'[2] writes former President of Médecins sans Frontières, Rony Brauman. Admittedly, humanitarian aid and mediation are two different things, though they do occasionally overlap, united as they are in their desire to limit suffering and as they participate in negotiations with belligerents to save lives in extreme situations. Humanitarian aid is defined as 'material and human assistance operations to help people suffering the repercussions of natural disasters and wars';[3] mediation, on the other hand, 'is a process in which a third party assists the disputants, with their consent, in preventing, managing, or resolving a conflict'.[4] It is this specific aspect of overlap that interests us, because it is here that acute moral issues also arise.

Before examining the borderline situations, it may be useful to distinguish between strong and weak mediators. Strong mediators are able to use their military, diplomatic and economic power to make their voices heard, if not obeyed. Looking back in history, this was the case of the papacy in the Catholic world for five centuries after the 1200s. The Church drew its force from the accumulation of its strengths, combining spiritual and temporal power with the capacity to make, interpret and apply laws. It had the extraordinary advantage of being a powerful mediator at a time when there were virtually no others.

For example, Pope Alexander VI—remembered chiefly for his orgy-filled life—mediated between Spain and Portugal, partitioning the world for the first time and thus averting a war between the two countries. Through him, Spain and Portugal concluded the Treaty of Tordesillas on 7 June 1494, dividing ownership of the new world being conquered between them alone, much to the chagrin of the world's other seafaring powers (French King Francis I is said to have exclaimed, in a reaction to the news of the treaty: 'The sun shines for me as it does for others.') Much more recently, the United States and Russia have mediated in the Middle East or in the former Soviet space respectively, using their political, military and economic power to bring the talks to a conclusion and make sure the results of their diplomatic efforts coincided with their geostrategic interests. Former US President Donald Trump provides a striking example: in violation of a Security Council resolution, he acquiesced to Morocco's demand that the United States recognise Moroccan sovereignty over the former

Spanish Sahara,[5] a price he paid for getting Morocco to normalise its relations with Israel in December 2020.

For the purposes of our discussion of ethical dilemmas, I will concentrate on weak mediators, for whom the sun never shines: they have no power to impose or to attract. By weak mediators, I refer to those from the United Nations, who, although they enjoy the legitimacy conferred on them by the UN Charter, remain subject to a generally divided Security Council; to countries such as Switzerland, Norway or even Qatar, which have specialised in this niche; and to the private mediation NGOs gradually emerging after 2000, which have no diplomatic legitimacy but which hold discreet talks with the belligerents in low- and medium-intensity conflicts.

Weak does not mean adrift. These mediators are not anchorless. They have an acknowledged moral capital and participate in the political environment they help shape; weak mediators are dependent on, but also the bearers of, norms and interests, a concept of their role and a vision of peace they must accommodate with the balance of power on the ground.

In Judeo-Christian culture, the mediator was initially a prophet (Moses) or quasi-divine figure (Christ) working for humanity's salvation. The mediator helped restore global order and the rules by which the world should be governed, in a desire to end war. Later, in Diderot and d'Alembert's 1751 *Encyclopédie*, 'mediator' was given its more current definition, with the introduction most importantly of two crucial terms—neutrality and impartiality—that provide the reference frame but also constitute an eternal dilemma: 'Sovereign or neutral State ...,	[the mediator] must be fair, impartial & a friend of peace ... in order to reconcile the minds of princes, which the furies of war have often too alienated to listen to reason or to want to discuss peace directly with each other.'[6]

Neutrality and impartiality are often linked and sometimes used interchangeably. Neutrality means being equidistant between two camps, while impartiality consists in acting without bias and completely independently to provide 'relief ... in proportion to need, and ... therefore not [even-handedly]'.[7] In a war that obeys the rules of chivalry, this wouldn't be a problem. But how can mediators remain neutral and impartial in the face of belligerents who violate international humanitarian law and its principles not to inflict unnecessary suffering and commit abuses against civilians? Can they 'do business' with the organisers of forced displacement and genocide without going over to 'the dark side'? To what extent should mediators agree to compromise their principles in order to limit the suffering of others? As I explain later, the question of neutrality varies widely depending on the nature of the mediators. The UN Security Council has established mandates for mediation that sometimes stray far from the definition of neutrality, as in the case of Syria (see Chapter 9). Mediation NGOs, owing to their weakness, may be more vulnerable to pressure from the belligerents. Interestingly, the Berghof Foundation has replaced the concept of impartiality with that of 'multi-partiality', to emphasise that the real challenge is to 'approach all parties with openness, trying to understand their underlying interests and motivations'.[8]

The initial challenge, though, is to put into practice the principles of action in dynamic environments where the space for mediation is never known in advance, a space that is the result of ongoing negotiations with belligerents looking to benefit, and which evolves according to the circumstances of the conflict, thus making it tricky for mediators to position themselves.

Mediators are inevitably used

Mediators exist only insofar as the belligerents stand to gain by their use. What do mediators bring to the table that might be of interest to the parties in conflict? The answer varies from situation to situation. Mediators are sources of information, regarding not only the demands and red lines of the enemy, but also the shifting positions of regional and international powers. They sometimes help the weaker party clarify its limits and prepare it for the technical aspects of the negotiations. They help set the agenda for talks, act as clerks, host negotiations in neutral locations, facilitate prisoner exchanges. Depending on the circumstances, they might also play the role of guarantors, formulate proposals in the form of 'non-papers'[9] and facilitate access to humanitarian aid.

In addition to the practical aspects, mediators also have symbolic and political power. They international-ise the conflict and give it visibility; they can help change the dynamics and the balance of power, and legitimise the parties. All this matters—the belligerents know it only too well and make sure to take advantage of it. Mediators, despite their best efforts to the con-trary, are sucked into the war, becoming indirect par-ticipants in it. They are themselves an object of negotiation on which the belligerents must agree and everyone will try to manipulate them, to exploit them—in short, to use them. Mediators must therefore accept that they will be used, but without allowing themselves to play the 'useful idiot'—that is to say, without being manipulated and utilised by a belligerent to deceive the enemy as to its intentions.

Only very rarely has a court considered the manipula-tion of a mediator. During the Nuremberg trials, Swedish businessman Johan Birger Essen Dahlerus[10] recounted how he was manipulated by 'his friend', Hermann Göring, the most powerful man in the Third Reich after Adolf Hitler, to deceive the British govern-ment about Germany's intentions and peel it away from its Polish ally by leading Britain to believe that war could be avoided. In the weeks preceding the war, Dahlerus shuttled back and forth between Berlin and London bearing German proposals. He met with British officials and with Prime Minister Neville Chamberlain. On 30 August 1939, the afternoon of the last day of peace (!), at Göring's instigation, Dahlerus made one last attempt to mediate between London and Berlin, once again in order to mislead the British about German intentions. Pushed to the point of exasperation during the Nuremberg trial by the British prosecutor, Sir David Maxwell Fyfe, Dahlerus admitted: 'I thought I could contribute something to prevent a new war ... but had I known what I know today, I would have realised that my efforts could not possibly succeed.'[11]

There is no place for naiveté in diplomatic games. For the belligerents, the pursuit of peace is no different from the conduct of hostilities. It is almost always a messy business, involving treachery, cheating, ruses and broken promises, and in which false hope alternates with real progress. The UN mediator for Libya, Ghassan Salamé, for example, was by his own admission 'stabbed in the back'[12] when some of the very countries, such as Russia, that had voted for the arms embargo in the Security Council sent boatloads of military equipment to the belligerents they were all the while supporting.

Mediators find themselves sitting at the table with leaders who have not needed to read Machiavelli's *The Prince* to 'be cunning as a fox and fierce as a lion' and who are almost always determined to stay in power.

Avoiding missteps

So how can mediators keep a steady course and avoid becoming complicit with the belligerents, despite their best intentions to the contrary? Paul Ricoeur has reflected on dealing with moral dilemmas in medicine, but his approach could be applied also to dilemmas arising for mediators in armed conflicts. Ricoeur suggests that, to avoid the pitfalls of rotten compromises, clinicians must define the rules by which they work not as the end in itself, but as a limit that must be immediately put to the test of the reality of the situation. This creates a tension, a back and forth between the rules and the reality, leading to what Ricoeur calls 'practical wisdom', a moral compass for action in 'situations of distress where the choice is not between good and bad, but between bad and worse'.[13] Ricoeur invokes the vision of Immanuel Kant's categorical imperatives,[14] (that a truly good act can become a universal law) and challenges this to bring it into confrontation with the particular circumstances affecting people's lives. In other words, Ricoeur poses the norm as a horizon, reflects on its concrete consequences in a specific situation and, in all conscience, aims to identify the least bad option; this is how he arrives at the least of all evils. For Ricoeur, 'practical wisdom' implies deliberations between 'wise and competent' men and women who might lessen the arbitrary nature of the moral judgement, and that 'the conviction sealing the decision then benefits from the multifaceted character of the debate'. In more operational terms, the decision arises from the confrontation between two poles—the principles (of neutrality and of impartiality) and the potential consequences (peace or war, protection or suffering)—and the belief that thoughtful, open-minded deliberation may limit the risk of missteps, that such careful debate could weigh the principles against their real-life tangible effects.

But in real life, immediate choices hardly appear as black-and-white terms as they might once the fog of war has lifted and with the space and time to look back, perhaps more objectively and with more information than was available to us at the time. In the heat of the moment, risks and opportunities must be considered, many of them traps, and with constant uncertainty about the belligerents' behaviour or their aims. Only feedback and the process of deliberation can minimise the dangers of a decision that will affect entire populations. All the more so as, when it comes to armed-conflict mediation, there are neither infallible markers nor immovable red lines, only dynamic situations that oblige us to re-evaluate yesterday's choices in the light of the changing circumstances and the political and military balance of power. Mediators must weigh all these considerations if they are not to become an instrument in the hands of the oppressors.

To what extent should mediators ignore human rights violations when they talk with the belligerents, on the grounds that raising the violations risks undermining their peace efforts and threatens humanitarian access? To what extent should they commit to relieve suffering, even if this means participating in a policy of forced displacement?[15]

In this second part, I will consider how the question of the ethical limits of mediators and the interpretation of neutrality and impartiality come up repeatedly, and how they are reinterpreted, in borderline situations.

The first example that I examine, however, is drawn not from the action of a specific mediator, but from a specific moment in the action—or rather, the non-action—of the International Committee of the Red Cross (ICRC) during the Second World War, a non-action often interpreted as a rotten compromise during an ongoing extermination operation. This tragic moment in European history has helped shape the framework for reflection on both humanitarian action and the mediator's work to this day. I will review the internal debate that took place within the International Committee on a single decisive day, 14 October 1942, when each member used moral principles and consequential analyses to justify his or her attitude and/or 'neutrality'. Subsequent criticism of this situation paved the way for the discussion in the 1990s of the definition of neutrality in the face of mass violence—a discussion that went far beyond the ICRC and which continues to influence mediation practices, including during the genocide in Rwanda in

1994, when ICRC delegate Philippe Gaillard referred to this precedent to explain his decision to remain on the spot despite all the risks incurred, saving 70,000 Tutsis and reading aloud from Arthur Rimbaud's *A Season in Hell* every night to his team.[16]

Next I consider two other borderline cases involving United Nations mediation, the first taking place during the war in Bosnia-Herzegovina (1992–1995), when the United States was at the height of its power. The United Nations had a mandate to protect populations and could have intervened through what was at the time uncontested Western military power; however, it refrained from doing so, refusing to distinguish between aggressors and those they assaulted, in the name of a certain reading of neutrality. This example is emblematic, because it testifies to the insidious process by which the UN went from compromise to rotten compromise, wanting to do good at each stage but, in the end, provoking the worst crime against humanity committed on European soil since the Second World War.

The other case involves UN mediation activities in 2012 in Syria, i.e. at the crossroads of two eras, when the United States was still engaged in a policy of regime change and believed that it controlled the international system, only to run headlong into Russian opposition. Supported by China and many other governments, Russia challenged norms that the Western world held to be universal, a challenge that limited the space for mediation and humanitarian work, and which sparked fresh, tragic dilemmas.

Each of these cases will tell us something about the dilemma implicit in the choices to be made, the tension between compromise and rotten compromises, and will force us to test the principles of neutrality and impartiality, even if this means ultimately abandoning them.

7

NEUTRALITY IN THE FACE OF GENOCIDE

Can one remain neutral and impartial in the face of mass violence? The worlds of mediation and humanitarian action have grappled with that question since their inception, albeit from different angles. One especially dire case arose during the Second World War, at the International Committee of the Red Cross (ICRC). The precedent set at that time has come to frame the debate for humanitarians, as it sheds a harsh light on the dilemmas they currently face in borderline situations.

'Neutrality' is a crucial concept for the ICRC; founded in February 1863, it is the oldest of humanitarian organisations; however, and even though its work is predicated on the concept of neutrality, the ICRC long used the term but did not define it. Neutrality was mentioned at its first international conference, in October 1863, with a view to affording some protection to ambulances, military hospitals, medical personnel and the wounded during conflicts. A year later, the term 'neutral' was used in Article 1 of the Geneva Convention for the Amelioration of the Condition of the Wounded in Armies in the Field, adopted on 22 August 1864. But beyond its application to protect hospitals, the wounded and medical personnel, the concept of neutrality remained unclear for the ICRC.

It was not until 1936 that Max Huber, then president of the ICRC and also one of its great ideologues, defined neutrality in a context of mounting international tension: Hitler, Stalin and Mussolini were already in power. Italy had invaded Ethiopia the year before, gassing civilian populations in violation of international law. Japan had occupied Manchuria in 1931 and was preparing to expand its occupation in the rest of China. And in 1936 the Third Reich enacted its anti-Semitic laws. It was as those storm clouds were gathering that Huber wrote an article[1] in which he spelled out for the first time what he meant by neutrality, and defined the concept as 'an essential principle' of the ICRC.

Huber started by linking the ICRC's neutrality to 'the age-long neutrality of Switzerland', because, he explained, Swiss neutrality would allow the ICRC, which 'consist[ed] of Swiss nationals and had its headquarters in Switzerland', to continue its work in time of war. His strict definition of neutrality laid the foundation of humanitarian action and was a guarantee of its effectiveness:

All this humanitarian work must be done for the benefit of everyone without distinction and under all circumstances, that is to say, even in the gravest eventuality—that of war—when men are so tragically tempted to choose one side or the other. If the Red Cross is to be able to offer its help to everyone and to do its work in centres which are utterly different from, or even hostile to, one another, the Red Cross must inspire everywhere a feeling of complete moral security and maintain everywhere relations of mutual confidence. ... At the same time, even when dealing with breaches of the Conventions or with any act that is a violation of humanitarian principles, the International Red Cross Committee has no intention whatsoever of sitting in judgment. It is not a court of justice and, besides, it has not itself the means of ascertaining the facts, which alone would enable it to give a verdict.[2]

Huber observed that the ICRC had no means to impose the rules of which it is the guardian. While conceding that the organisation was powerless, he endeavoured to transform its impotence into an asset: the ICRC should not take sides and should make no moral judgements, in order to protect its effectiveness. That was his message— and it was endorsed by the vice-president of the ICRC, Carl Burckhardt.

The call to abstain from moral judgement took on particular significance in August 1942. The representative of the World Jewish Congress, Gerhart Riegner, informed Burckhardt, his former professor of law at the Graduate Institute of International Studies in Geneva, of the existence of a general plan to exterminate the Jews of Europe. Burckhardt, the equivalent of the ICRC's foreign minister, was just as well if not better informed about the real meaning of the 'Final Solution'. But he had no intention of approaching the German government, doubtless in the belief that defending the racially persecuted was a lost cause that might cause fresh problems with an already difficult interlocutor. In fact, Burckardt, the former League of Nations High Commissioner for the Free City of Danzig and a fervent Germanophile,[3] had other priorities. He had long been worried about the communist threat hanging over Europe and the world; in his eyes, that was a much more serious menace than Hitlerism, which he dismissed as little more than an unpleasant episode. In late 1941, under cover of his activities as vice-president of the ICRC, he travelled to London in an attempt to lay the foundations for a separate peace between the German conservatives[4] and the British. Burckardt had contacts in London and was close to the former Foreign Secretary, Lord Halifax. But Halifax was no longer powerful. In January 1941 he had been appointed British ambassador in Washington, having fallen from grace in late May 1940, when, as the German forces were approaching the English Channel and the British and French armies were defeated, he had proposed that Mussolini be approached to explore the terms of peace negotiations with Hitler. Halifax clashed with Winston Churchill and was finally overruled during stormy sessions in the war cabinet, where Churchill imposed the need to continue fighting.

Churchill was suspicious of Burckhardt, whom he considered pro-German, and he definitely did not want to have Stalin believe that the Anglo-Americans were ready to make a pact with the Third Reich.

With the exception of Burckhardt, the members of the ICRC executive committee[5] were truly ill at ease about the persecution of Jews, even though the news reaching them was incomplete. The committee remained a closed circle of some twenty co-opted notables with conservative ideals and who, above all, analysed the twentieth century using the intellectual tools of the nineteenth.[6] Their organisation was close to the Swiss authorities, linking the Swiss policy of neutrality and the humanitarian vocation of the country. What should they do? The term 'genocide' had yet to be coined (in 1943 by the Polish lawyer Raphael Lemkin)[7] to describe the extermination of a group of humans, but this in no way prevented the organisation from thinking about the possibilities for relief activities. In July 1942 the ICRC executive committee asked jurist Jean Pictet to draw up a draft public appeal. Pictet (who later was instrumental in drafting the 1949 Geneva Conventions) produced several versions, the last of which was accepted but did not, in his view, go anywhere near far enough: 'toothless, in other words, it did not pack enough punch, it was too soft, not demanding enough, ... it had been completely emasculated'.[8]

Titled 'Call for the application of the essential principles of international law relating to the conduct of hostilities', every word of the draft was carefully weighed so as to strike a balance between criticism of the two camps and not appear unneutral. The plight of the racial deportees was the real issue, but it was bundled with other subjects so as not to upset the authorities in Berlin. Although the appeal denounced four breaches of international law, it took the additional precaution of referring to neither Israelites nor Jews. The first breaches, which naturally targeted the Third Reich, concerned the deportation of Jews and the indiscriminate aerial bombardment of cities, in particular Cologne, Essen and Bremen, between May and June 1942, for which the American and British air forces were responsible. It also raised two other subjects: the impact on people of economic warfare and the prisoners of war who were denied the protection of the 1929 Geneva Convention[9] (specifically, Soviet prisoners held by the Germans and vice versa).

At the end of August 1942, Max Huber communicated the draft to his colleagues on the committee, for their views 'on the advisability of such an appeal in the present circumstances'. He was surprised by the number of supportive written replies that reached headquarters at the end of September. He had thought the appeal might be rejected, because even if drafted in cautious terms, it would risk upsetting Berlin; thus, to his consternation, and that of Burckhardt, a majority of Committee members were in favour (twelve out of nineteen, plus two abstentions).[10] Both Huber and Burckhardt preferred 'cautious neutrality', fearing that indignation would be futile and tarnish the ICRC's reputation for impartiality and neutrality.

The meeting of 14 October 1942 was decisive, with Committee members heavily influenced by developments on the ground: Switzerland was surrounded by the Axis powers; Germany had conquered almost all of Europe; and the outcome of the war remained uncertain both on the eastern front, where the Battle of Stalingrad had been raging since 17 July, and to the west, with the United States' entry into the war on 7 December 1941 after the Japanese bombing of Pearl Harbor. Nazi Germany and Fascist Italy might still triumph. It was against this backdrop that the committee cautiously deliberated the persecution of the Jews and the ICRC's role to protect the persecuted.

The Committee's deliberations focused on the same basic issues as I am discussing in this book: impartiality and neutrality, the terms related but not synonymous. For the ICRC, impartiality means coming to the aid of victims according to their needs, while neutrality means not taking sides. Both terms are crucial, because they raise a fundamental question: how to arbitrate between the rule, i.e. the principle of neutrality ('abstention from all moral judgement', to use Max Huber's formula), and mass persecution. Would 'abstention from all moral judgement' make the ICRC a silent accomplice?

It may be useful to recall the legal and political context of the time. The 1929 Geneva Convention protected prisoners of war but did not mention the protection of civilians. The ICRC nevertheless had a right of initiative with regard to violations of international law. Max Huber had discussed the importance of that right (i.e. the right to draw the attention of the international community to violations of international humanitarian law) in his 1936 article. The ICRC, he wrote, 'has, moreover, the right of initiative and can itself take in hand certain cases about which no complaint has been made but which, in its opinion, justify its spontaneous intervention'.[11] During the first two years of the war, the ICRC twice expressed public concern about the plight of civilian populations.[12]

As surprising as it may seem for an organisation declaring itself to be independent, the then President of the Swiss Confederation, Philipp Etter, was also a member of the Committee. Not only did Etter actively participate in the deliberations of 14 October (he exceptionally made the trip from Bern to participate in the meeting),[13] he was also fiercely opposed to the appeal, which he feared would undermine Swiss neutrality vis-à-vis Berlin. A member of the Christian-Democrat party, Etter supported a decidedly conservative, adaptable and friendly policy toward Nazi Germany and fascist Italy. Etter acted as if the ICRC were an emanation of Switzerland and as if the decisions it was called upon to take would inevitably affect his country. His conflicting positions as both head of state and Committee member mirrored this conflation of politics and humanitarian action, and reduced the ICRC's room to manoeuvre. How could the organisation claim to be independent when a head of state was part of its executive body? The situation was akin to that faced by UN mediators which I will describe later, insofar as the latter depend closely on the UN Secretary-General and even more on the Security Council, a political body if ever there was one.

So what happened on 14 October? In the salons of the former Hôtel Métropole, and in a departure from the Committee's usual proceedings, everyone was given the opportunity, one by one, to express their point of view, without debate. The minutes show that the majority (thirteen out of twenty-two) were in favour of the appeal, on several grounds. First and foremost, supporters did not believe that the belligerents would turn against the ICRC, because the organisation was delivering, on a reciprocal basis, millions of parcels to prisoners of war protected by the Geneva Conventions. They deemed the risk to the ICRC as low to non-existent. They also feared that the moral values upheld by the ICRC would be betrayed should it not issue the appeal. Renée-Marguerite Frick-Cramer, a Swiss legal scholar, humanitarian activist and the first woman to sit on the governing body of an international organisation, was particularly eloquent:

The Appeal will certainly not harm the practical work of the Red Cross, which has been useful to the belligerents on the basis of reciprocity. [On the other hand], the Committee's silence would be a negative act of extremely serious import and risks compromising the Committee's very existence. The Red Cross may disappear in the international turmoil, but this must not be because it has turned its back on the moral and spiritual values on which it was founded.[14]

Considered in the light of Paul Ricoeur's 'practical wisdom' approach, the two main arguments in favour of issuing the appeal were both normative and consequentialist;[15] normative in that silence on the part of the ICRC was tantamount to complicity, a betrayal of the values underpinning its work and of its raison d'être, especially since both sides benefitted from its activities for prisoners of war and the risk was therefore negligible.

Conversely, the appeal's opponents considered that the appeal 'could undermine the humanitarian work of the ICRC'. Etter was concerned 'that, as the war runs on, the belligerents will become more sensitive. As a result, they will construe the appeal as a judgement and if they are offended by it, it will already have failed in its purpose'.[16] He feared that the appeal would be exploited by one of the belligerents for propaganda purposes, placing the ICRC in a difficult position. He added: 'Moreover, the appeal could undermine the practical activities of the Committee, which constitute its essential work. After all, the work of the good Samaritan is known only because of his actions.' But Etter did not define what he meant by 'actions'. Other members of the Committee who opposed the draft underscored the risk 'that an appeal from a neutral country might offend the belligerents engaged in a total war and devoting all their energy to ensuring victory'.

The opponents' arguments were also normative, although they tended to emphasise the consequences of a possible appeal for Switzerland rather than for the ICRC. Speaking out would have a negative impact on Switzerland for a very uncertain gain. Where the appeal's supporters stressed the need to remain true to the organisation's values, its opponents pointed out that it would be overstepping the principle of neutrality to stand in judgement of the criminal actions of belligerents.

While most of the Committee members were in favour of an appeal, they did not vote on the principle of its publication but rather on how to transmit it to Berlin. On that point, they had clearly not coordinated their views and remained divided on how to proceed. Should the ICRC send out a circular letter? Should it assess its work during the war, referencing the points raised in the appeal? Approach the parties confidentially? All of this ultimately prompted Edouard Chapuisat, rapporteur of the meeting and himself hostile to the issuance of the appeal, to say 'that nobody was in favour of sending the appeal in the form in which it was considered'.[17] The view that there should be no appeal prevailed; there was no majority for how it should be sent. The decision was a great relief to President Etter as well as to Carl Burckhardt, who opposed any form of public protest and stressed the organisation's necessary 'neutrality'. The final tally was significant from more than one point of view: all the members originally from Geneva but one (the poet, librettist and novelist Jacques Chenevière, the scion of a patrician family) voted in favour, because they identified more closely with the organisation, whereas all those not originally from Geneva but one (Swiss bibliophile, scholar and collector Martin Bodmer) voted against, no doubt because they were more concerned about protecting Switzerland's interests than the ICRC's mission; thus, the linkages between the Swiss government and the ICRC presidency played a decisive role in ensuring that the views of the minority prevailed. To use the terms of Paul Ricoeur, while deliberations took place, they were swayed by the direct influence of government policy and by the presidency of the ICRC. In methodological terms, to limit the risk of complicity, deliberations must be free and, whenever possible, unaffected by the internal balance of power in an organisation. This is far easier said than done, because it implies that the will and ability exist to create a space for deliberation shielded from the institution's internal power relations. However difficult that may be to achieve, this lesson remains extremely relevant for both humanitarians and mediators.

I have focused here on the discussion of the appeal in 1942. Why then, two years later, in the final months of the war, when the outcome was no longer in doubt and there was no longer any threat to Switzerland, did the International Committee not revisit the matter? Count Bernadotte, President of the Swedish Red Cross, had convinced Nazi officials to release several thousand Scandinavian prisoners in the last weeks of the war. If he could do it, why could the ICRC not have tried to approach the Third Reich again on the 'Jewish question'. Many years later, in 2002, ICRC Director of International Law François Bugnon commented on his organisation's policy during the Second World War: 'It was a painful failure, because the ICRC remained a prisoner of its traditional modes of operation; it did not take—or did not want to take—the full measure of the tragedy that was unfolding, and did not know how to deal with it by reversing the order of its priorities and by taking the initiatives and risks required in the situation.'[18]

In the 1990s, United Nations mediators would also have the opportunity to reflect on how they construed neutrality when confronted with borderline situations, forcing them to redefine their norms and values while knowing that compromising with perpetrators of war crimes would undermine their moral authority. How could the UN claim to act as a mediator if it betrayed the very moral basis undergirding its activities? Pursuing without result a mediation with belligerents who are known war criminals is a problematic business because it lends them international legitimacy and maintains a sham peace process. Mediation then risks becoming a form of complicity, even collusion. These were the challenges facing UN mediation in Bosnia-Herzegovina in the 1990s and more recently in Syria, dispelling the comforting notion that mediators are necessarily on the side of good and virtue.

8

BOSNIA

FAREWELL TO NEUTRALITY

From the former Yugoslavia to Africa's Great Lakes region, from Syria to Ukraine, the world of mediation has had to come to grips with the issue of neutrality in the face of often violent, grave crimes. The experience of the United Nations in Bosnia-Herzegovina in the early 1990s brought a new level of awareness that the principle of neutrality must not be used to justify turning one's back on threatened populations.

The slippery slope from compromise to rotten compromise is both perverse and insidious, so gradual as to be almost imperceptible. It involves multiple tiny steps, none of which is in and of itself inherently bad and each of which is intended to be useful, even to do good. In the case of Bosnia, all of these steps taken together resulted in the greatest crime committed on European soil since the end of the Second World War: the July 1995 Srebrenica massacre, when more than 8,000 men were murdered by Bosnian Serb forces in a so-called 'UN safe area'. At the time, Western governments refused to set their minds to war, even though public opinion, revolted by what it was seeing and hearing on TV and radio, by what it was reading in the papers, demanded that they act; thus, on the proposal of France, Britain and the United States, the Security Council resolved this contradiction by adopting a deluge of resolutions,[1] reinforcing the UN's mandate to the point that the organisation was transformed into a force to protect Muslim populations under siege, but without the will to implement it.[2] The member countries of the Security Council held out promises that they were unable to keep, which led to the tragedy of forced displacements of women and children and the deaths of thousands of men in mass executions in Srebrenica.

Let us remember the context: this was the era of the single American superpower, of the myth of the 'end of history'. Yet the United States held that Bosnia was none of its business. In the words of then US Secretary of State James Baker, 'We don't have a dog in this fight',[3] words that stymied any action until after the Srebrenica massacre, when the very credibility of NATO was itself jeopardised. In the meantime, before the US intervened, it fell to Europe and the United Nations, which were mediating jointly between the Serbs, the Croats and the Bosnians, to put an end to the conflict.

In the initial phase of the war, the UN intervened militarily, through its peacekeeping force (UNPROFOR);

diplomatically, through its joint mediation with the European Community; judicially, tasking its international judges to prosecute war criminals; and finally, through its humanitarian action. On paper, the multidimensional approach made sense but the shock of Srebrenica would be all the greater as the UN thought it had employed effectively all the means to restore peace.

In reality, the United Nations was caught in a trap of its own making, ensnared between the pursuit of justice and the pursuit of peace. Had the International Criminal Tribunal for the former Yugoslavia (ICTY) indicted the main perpetrators of war crimes and crimes against humanity, including Serbian President Slobodan Milosevic, it would have simultaneously 'torpedoed' the peace conference being held in Geneva. How could peace be achieved if one of the crucial protagonists was unable to participate in the conference because he had been indicted for international crimes? Moreover, Western governments, which provided the bulk of the UN peace-keeping forces, were concerned about the safety of their troops. A pro-active ICTY prosecutor might pave the way for reprisals against the UN's iconic 'Blue Helmets'.[4] As a result, until Srebrenica, the ICTY indicted only small fry—notwithstanding Prosecutor Richard Goldstone's rhetorical intention 'to oppose a peace concluded by devious war criminals who flout every prescription and fundamental norm of international law'.[5]

With justice side-lined, the peace conference, mediated by the United Nations and the European Community, was running on empty, unsupported by the Americans, let alone the Russians. The mediators were weak and complained bitterly: 'What we lack is clout.'[6] The belligerents had no desire to conclude a peace agreement: the Bosnian Serbs were too strong, the Muslims and the Croats too feeble—never a good combination for successful mediation. The Bosnian Serbs were winning the war and had little incentive to negotiate. In the Security Council they were backed by Russia. The authorities in Sarajevo and Zagreb, for their part, were hoping for a NATO intervention that would 'turn the tables' and did not want to negotiate from a position of weakness. And although the UN and the EC were encouraged by Washington, the US had no troops on the ground. So between the military victories on one side and the wait for a providential saviour on the other, the peace conference stalled; all the while the number of war crimes rose, in particular thanks to the pursuit of 'ethnic cleansing' policies.

One of the questions facing the mediators here, and in many other contexts, was the point at which mediation no longer made sense, at which it became an alibi for non-action. Earlier I gave the example of Birger Dahlerus, whom the Nazis used as a decoy. Dahlerus was a weak mediator without any leverage. Conversely, Nelson Mandela, exasperated by the obstructive tactics of certain Burundian parties and with the support of the African Union and of the international community to mediate in the Burundian civil war in 2000, threatened to withdraw and publicly denounce the blockage. His threat paid off: the government and around twenty political parties signed the Peace Accord on 28 August 2000 in Arusha, Tanzania. Leverage had been key; it was missing in the early 1990s for the UN and EC tandem of mediators in the former Yugoslavia.

In Bosnia-Herzegovina, on 16 April 1993, the United Nations was given a specific mandate under Chapter VII of its charter: to deploy force to protect Muslim populations in 'UN safe areas', which included in this case the capital, Sarajevo, as well as Srebrenica, Zepa, Gorazde and Bihac.[7] In other words, the United Nations had given itself a legitimate right to distinguish between the aggressor and the attacked and to wage war on the Bosnian Serb forces if civilian populations were attacked. The UN thus deployed thousands of Blue Helmets and was prepared to call on NATO air power, which controlled the skies.

However, the mandate stood in contradiction to the entire genetic make-up of the United Nations—its culture and its constant search for compromise (however ambiguous), which would have required it to switch from a mindset of interposition to one of confrontation. The UN would have had to admit that mediation no longer made sense in the circumstances, that it was nothing more than a futile form of shadow boxing. The countries sending contingents of Blue Helmets, including two permanent members of the Security Council (France and the UK), would have had to accept that there would be casualties. It would have meant being consistent with the mandate that the UN Security Council had adopted, under the impetus of Western governments. It would also have meant abandoning the principle of neutrality. No one was ready for that.

Dirty hands?

Having failed on three fronts simultaneously—judicial, diplomatic and military—the international community shifted its focus to humanitarian action. In what was an unprecedented logistical success, the United Nations airlifted 160,000 tonnes of food to Sarajevo and fed hundreds of thousands over the course of three years. Hundreds of trucks marked with the emblems of the Office of the United Nations High Commissioner for Refugees (UNHCR) and other humanitarian organisations criss-crossed Bosnia-Herzegovina, braving checkpoints, threats, various forms of pressure and the snipers targeting their teams, and the belligerent's attempts to divert the food.

The UNHCR and the ICRC faced a profound ethical dilemma: should they evacuate populations to save lives, but which would in essence fulfil the aim of a belligerent to the point of risking becoming complicit in the war crime of ethnic cleansing (forced deportation)? Or should they obey the principles of international law and refuse to cooperate with this policy, a refusal that would risk the loss of life, as a result of inaction? The dramatic situation in the former Yugoslavia was also proving to be a worrying testing ground for modern warfare. It anticipated other situations, such as in Syria, where 'social and demographic engineering'[8] (the European Union's chilling description), would be widely used by the Assad regime twenty years later. How should humanitarian organisations position themselves in the face of ethnic cleansing if the Blue Helmets could only stand by and if international justice and mediation were powerless? Should they participate in forced displacements in order to make them more humane? At what point do they cross the line into complicity or even collusion?

At the beginning of Chapter 6, I referred to Paul Ricoeur and the need to weigh the rule in the light of unique circumstances and respect for others. But can respect for others—the desire to save them—also force the opposite, namely a pact with 'the ethnic cleanser'? As Larry Hollingworth and Tony Land, who were then in charge of UNHCR operations, put it, 'The only real question we had to answer was whether to act or to leave with clean hands, having done nothing. We wanted to save lives without becoming travel agents for the ethnic cleansers. It was a balance that was almost impossible to strike.'[9] Confronted by the same challenges, Jacques de Maio, ICRC coordinator in Bosnia-Herzegovina from 1993 to 1995, explained his own dilemma:

> We faced an ethical struggle. On the one hand, we wanted to protect people's physical integrity, but their evacuation was part of a policy of forced displacement, that is to say a clear violation of international humanitarian law. By doing good in the short term, i.e. by facilitating an evacuation in humane conditions, we were participating in an even greater evil in the long term, emptying the territories of their minorities.[10]

The two organisations opted for the short-term good.

Only once did a senior UN official, Sadako Ogata, preferring to have 'clean hands', make the opposite choice and remind the parties of the rules without worrying about the consequences. In February 1993, Ogata, the UN High Commissioner for Refugees, travelled to Bosnia to see the situation first-hand. Tony Land picked her up at Sarajevo airport in his bullet-proof car, which nonetheless had a huge hole from a sniper's bullet. He drove her to the UNHCR office, which had just been shelled and where one of the employees had been seriously injured. He tried to convince Ogata of the usefulness of the UNHCR's presence: 'Despite all the violations, we save lives.' A few days later, and to everyone's stupefaction, Ogata decided to withdraw the UNHCR from Bosnia, for the stated purpose of putting an end to the diversion of humanitarian aid, the blocking of convoys, the attacks and the constant acts of intimidation against the organisation by the belligerents. By her action, one of the rare cases where the head of a UN agency publicly confronted the warlords of the former Yugoslavia, she reminded them of the rules. Her decision to leverage humanitarian action paid off in the short term, but she was swiftly called to order by the UN Secretary-General, Boutros Boutros-Ghali, who considered her lack of faith in the Blue Helmets 'unacceptable' and, most importantly, that she should not have shown that the emperor had no clothes; yet, the merit of her action was to show that the belligerents knew what they were doing and had to be held responsible. The UNHCR immediately resumed its activities, but only after it had obtained assurances from the parties that they would temporarily loosen the humanitarian vice. The victory would be short-lived.

The road to Srebrenica

UN Security Council resolution 819, adopted on 16 April 1993, referred to Srebrenica several times, denouncing the 'deliberate armed attacks and shelling of the innocent civilian population' and demanding that 'all parties ... treat Srebrenica and its surroundings as a safe area which should be free from any armed attack or any other hostile act'. It also demanded 'the immediate cessation of armed attacks by Bosnian Serb paramilitary units against Srebrenica and their immediate withdrawal from the areas surrounding Srebrenica'. The resolution reaffirmed that 'any taking or acquisition of territory by the threat or use of force, including through the practice of "ethnic cleansing", is unlawful and unacceptable'.

In Srebrenica itself (independently of the negotiations in New York but also in April 1993), serious consideration was being given to evacuating the entire besieged population, i.e. roughly 40,000 people. The UNHCR even started to make logistical arrangements and the town's Muslim leaders, watching the vice slowly close on the enclave, scrambled frantically to ask the UNHCR to evacuate the entire population via Serb territory. Based in Sarajevo for the United Nations at the time, David Harland describes how the organisation, which had initially resolved to take part in the evacuation, then invoked international law to backtrack, refusing to act as a possible accomplice to a war crime:

> UNHCR contacted the local Serb commanders, who agreed [to the evacuation]. The first convoy of vehicles was prepared, and the first evacuees said their goodbyes, and the first vehicles began to move. And then it was stopped. The Bosnian government in Sarajevo, as well as foreign friends, said that the evacuation deal was unacceptable. For UNHCR to broker a deal with Serb generals and desperate Bosniacs to remove a whole population, contrary to the most basic precepts of

international humanitarian law, was just unacceptable. A deal like that would be nothing more than facilitating ethnic cleansing.[11]

As was tragically borne out by subsequent events, being party to a policy of ethnic cleansing would have constituted a lesser evil.

But it was in this context that 200 Dutch Blue Helmets were finally deployed in the vicinity of Srebrenica (Canada and Sweden refused to send any soldiers to participate in what they considered to be 'mission impossible').

In light of this, the Bosnian Serb attack on Srebrenica two years later could hardly have come as a surprise to the United Nations. Formally, the regions forming the Muslim enclaves had been placed under the protection of the United Nations as 'safe areas' since the adoption of resolution 819; however, in Srebrenica, the 200 Dutch Blue Helmets were quickly overwhelmed by Bosnian Serb forces. Neither the United Nations nor NATO air forces intervened, despite repeated requests for air support from the Dutch commander on the ground, whose Minister of Defence opposed any military intervention that would endanger the lives of his soldiers. His words to the United Nations left no room for doubt: he didn't want any Dutch soldiers returning home in body bags.

In a tragic reversal of roles, the most perverse effect of this decision was that the 'zero casualties' doctrine would give precedence to the protection of the Blue Helmets in Srebrenica over that of the population they were there to protect. In a cruel irony, a NATO air intervention would have been possible, even probable, had it not been necessary to protect the so-called protectors above all others. In the UN report on the fall of Srebrenica, Kofi Annan admits that the main UNPROFOR officials 'were all deeply reluctant to use air power', in part because they 'believed that by using air power against the Serbs we would be perceived as having entered the war against them, something not authorized by the Security Council and potentially fatal for a peacekeeping operation'.[12] That says it all.

At the end of the day, this international policy, with contradictory rules laid down then emptied of their substance, created an environment conducive to the worst possible outcome. On site, in Srebrenica, there were only a handful of international NGOs. One of the few to see the coming tragedy was Larry Hollingworth, a logistics officer with UNHCR: 'We knew that if the women were evacuated as the Bosnian Serbs intended, the area would become a zone for firing at will on the men who remained.' Although a few other internationals clung to the idea that the men would instead be sent to camps, Hollingworth's prediction came true. More than 8,000 men and adolescents over the age of sixteen were massacred over the course of a few days in July 1995.

It was after this mass crime that the United States finally intervened, first militarily, then diplomatically, because the credibility of the North Atlantic alliance was now at stake. If the Bosnian Serb forces could defeat the strongest military alliance in the world, what was the alliance worth? Hence NATO's decision to bomb Bosnian Serb forces and then have US Under-Secretary of State Richard Holbrooke take over and 'invite' all the parties to a peace conference. The conference was held at a military base in Dayton, Ohio (lending the final agreement its name), attended by the presidents of Serbia (Slobodan Milosevic), Croatia (Franjo Tudjman) and Bosnia-Herzegovina (Alija Izetbegovic). The peace thus imposed by the sole superpower at the time put an end to the hostilities. But it was in many respects a fragile and problematic peace: more than anything else, the Dayton Accords[13] froze the war, creating a dysfunctional state that was largely in the hands of nationalist parties at the heart of Europe—with the risk that the situation would eventually degenerate into a new conflict.

Learning from failure

During both the Srebrenica massacre and the genocide in Rwanda, Kofi Annan was the head of UN peacekeeping operations. When he was elected UN Secretary-General in 1997 one of the first things he did was to address, before the Rwandan parliament, the failings of the United Nations. He also signed a report acknowledging UN responsibility in the massacres in Srebrenica and commissioned another report on the genocide in Rwanda,[14] at the end of which he apologised for both tragedies. In his *mea culpa*, he acknowledged that the UN's 'errors [of judgement were] rooted in a philosophy of impartiality and non-violence wholly unsuited to the conflict in Bosnia'.[15] His report on the fall of Srebrenica underscored 'the pervasive ambivalence within the United Nations regarding the role of force in the pursuit of peace'.[16] In fact, for the UN, taking radical decisions, abiding by the consequences of dozens of Security Council resolutions and opting to use force to execute them stood in stark contradiction to the culture of an organisation that sees itself, above all else, as a forum representing some 200 states.

Annan wrote, in conclusion: 'The cardinal lesson of Srebrenica is that a deliberate and systematic attempt to terrorize, expel or murder an entire people must be met decisively with all necessary means, and with the political will to carry the policy through to its logical conclusion. ... the international community tried to reach a negotiated settlement with an unscrupulous and murderous regime.'[17]

The war in Bosnia-Herzegovina and the genocide of the Tutsis in Rwanda forced the United Nations to profoundly rethink and to abandon the principle of neutrality, which in light of both tragedies became synonymous with spinelessness, if not also downright cowardice. As Kofi Annan told the Rwandan parliament, 'In the face of genocide, there can be no standing aside, no looking away, no neutrality. There are perpetrators and there are victims; there is evil and there is evil's harvest.'[18]

But is the problem really the word 'neutrality'?

Neutrality served, in these instances, only to mask divisions within the UN Security Council and to delay a decision to conclude what turned out to be futile mediation, thus, prolonging the abuses being perpetrated by the belligerents. Ending the mediation would have had the benefit of clarifying the situation, at the risk of being interpreted as the abandonment of the victims in the pursuit of war. It also would have laid bare the fact that no government was willing to have its peace-keepers die for Bosnia.

Ultimately, attempts at mediation must end if the presence of mediators begins to serve as a smokescreen, allowing belligerents (who have no real desire to conclude a peace agreement) to perpetuate war crimes while the mediation continues.

9

SYRIA

MISSION IMPOSSIBLE

As in Bosnia, the conflict in Syria posed a dramatic dilemma for mediators: were they saving lives or were they accomplices to a policy of 'demographic engineering' (population transfers) carried out by a criminal regime in a conflict that saw both sides committing its share of horrors? Were the mediators complicit in war crimes, as suggested in a report by a UN independent fact-finding commission? If four-hundred thousand Syrians lost their lives between 2011 and 2021 and half the population, or roughly twelve million men, women and children were internally displaced or exiled as refugees: what was the point of UN mediation?

To answer these questions, I must return briefly to the watershed moment that marked the end of Pax Americana and the start of a new era bracketed by NATO's military intervention in Libya in 2011 and the civil war in Syria. Citing the Libyan precedent, Russia challenged the principle of the responsibility to protect populations in danger, international human rights and criminal justice, arguing that these were tools of Western interference (see Chapter 5).

The neutrality of the mediation mandate was a matter of dispute from the start in Syria. Contrary to custom, the UN Security Council's goal for its mediators was to help form an interim transitional government,[1] i.e. a power-sharing agreement between the autocratic Assad regime and the fragmented opposition, leading to democratic elections. The result of the mediation effort was therefore predetermined: the desire, if not the demand, that Bashar al-Assad give up power. The Syrian opposition, the Arab League and Western governments[2] wanted 'regime change'. But the Assad government wanted the exact opposite: to remain in power, and Russian military support for the regime radically modified the balance of power. It forced mediators to adapt to the new situation, and to this day they have sought in vain to conclude an agreement between the government and the opposition.

The fact that the anticipated political outcome of the mediation had been pre-determined by the international community constituted an additional challenge for a mediation effort perceived from the beginning as lacking impartiality. The Arab League,[3] initially a co-mediator with the UN, suspended Syria as a member, sending the signal that the mediation was biased. Following the

Assad regime's 2011 crackdown in the wake of peaceful protests, Western countries shuttered their embassies in Damascus, further weakening the mediation effort and further radicalising the regime. The first mediator, former UN Secretary-General Kofi Annan, stuck it out until August 2012, at which point he said, 'At a time when [...] the Syrian people desperately need action there continues to be finger-pointing and name-calling in the Security Council'.[4] Lakhdar Brahimi, a former Algerian Minister of Foreign Affairs and long-time UN diplomat, took over from Annan but was in turn prompted to resign by the deteriorating relations between Washington and Moscow following Russia's invasion of Crimea in 2014. With the subsequent appointment of the third mediator, Staffan de Mistura, a former Italian government minister and a UN diplomat, the UN alone was in charge of talks during the most ruthless fighting in Syria, between July 2014 and November 2018.

Each mediator faced the same difficulty: despite this being an internationalised civil war, they had no real political support from the regional or international players involved and no entry points on which to anchor a strategy in a zero-sum game situation. Each camp was ready to make the population suffer to impose its will and at times escalate the conflict. External parties contributed to radicalising the positions of the belligerents, including in the indirect confrontation between the United States and Russia.

In the wake of the 'Arab Spring' (a series of anti-government protests, uprisings and armed rebellions that spread across much of the Arab world in the early 2010s in response to corruption and economic stagnation), Syrians were themselves, in 2011, emboldened to protest—at first peacefully—chanting for the departure of their president. When those protests were violently put down, many of them switched to armed rebellion, setting in motion a vicious cycle of violence. Dozens of armed groups that were hostile to the government, including the Islamic State (Daesh), managed to occupy large swaths of the country, and though all sides committed countless war crimes, Daesh and pro-government forces stood out for their brutality. According to the Independent International Commission of Inquiry on Syria, 'In 2012, pro-Government forces began laying sieges in a coordinated and planned manner, aimed at forcing populations, collectively, to starve or surrender.'[5] On 30 August 2013, US President Obama decided not to order strikes against the Syrian regime, even though it had used sarin gas to kill hundreds of people in Ghouta, a suburb of Damascus—an act that crossed his self-proclaimed red line in the sand and which should have triggered action. From Washington's perspective, the Assad regime had become the lesser evil in the face of the rise of Islamic State.

For the price of its failure to act, Washington obtained the approval of UN Security Council resolution 2118, which repeated the terms of a communiqué drafted on 30 June 2012, laying down the principle of a government of national unity that included members of the opposition. It also obtained the resumption of talks at the 'Geneva II' conference in January 2014, which were fruitless, especially in the face of Russian military support of the Assad regime, reversing the balance of power and allowing Assad's government to retake most of its territory.

By the time UN special envoy Staffan de Mistura took up the reins of the international mediation effort, the situation had become catastrophic: the flight of millions of Syrians from their homeland was compounded by countless abuses of human rights by all sides. As the internationally recognised power, the Syrian government controlled international humanitarian aid while simultaneously starving the population in the besieged cities it was bombarding. Diplomatically, the situation had reached a total impasse, with none of the parties involved (including dozens of armed groups, the regime, Russia, Iran, Turkey, Saudi Arabia, the United States and Qatar) seriously engaged in any form of mediation.

The chimera of local ceasefires

In a valiant effort to help resolve the situation, de Mistura began criss-crossing Syria to engage with as many players as possible over the course of forty days.

Influenced by a report[6] by the Centre for Humanitarian Dialogue, one of the few mediation NGOs that had a team on the ground, he reversed the top-down approach used in vain by Kofi Annan and Lakhdar Brahimi. A few months earlier, in May 2014, a local agreement between the authorities and the opposition had been concluded under the aegis of the Iranian ambassador: after three years of siege, some 2,000 rebels had left the old city of Homs with their Kalashnikovs and their families in an evacuation supervised by the United Nations. Citing this precedent, de Mistura explained his plan of action to the UN Security Council and to the media in October 2014: to gradually restore peace from the bottom up. Given the country's fragmentation and specific local dynamics, the conflict would be 'frozen' at the local level, in the hope that peace would ripple out in virtuous circles, first locally and then nationally.[7] He used an aquatic metaphor: 'Many drops can produce a lake and a lake can produce a sea.'[8] De Mistura intended to pull the rug out from under Daesh's feet, stabilise Syria and avoid a regional explosion. He hoped this strategy would strike a chord and repeat 'the Sarajevo coup', by making Aleppo, the country's second-largest city but also an icon of multiculturalism, 'a safe area' (words that were never uttered, to avoid any reference to the disastrous precedent of Srebrenica).

The idea was that, under UN auspices, local ceasefires would lead to the establishment of neutral interim authorities and bring an end to suffering by paving the way for a process of reconciliation. But in early 2015, Syrian troops engaged in a fresh campaign of intensive shelling of Aleppo and starved the population to eliminate the opposition. Russia backed them up by also pounding the besieged city from the air.

While the United Nations mediation effort remained predicated on the concept of a democratic transition and the holding of 'free and fair' elections,[9] Russia, together with Turkey and Iran, adopted a radically different approach, outside the United Nations: they launched the 'Astana Process', as Kazakhstan was politically close to all three countries. The Astana Process did not seek a political solution; instead, it aimed to reduce the number of military confrontations with a view to enabling the authorities in Damascus to reclaim territories.[10] It led, in May 2017, to the establishment of four 'de-escalation zones' with the planned introduction of a ceasefire. The level of violence fell temporarily, which had the unfortunate consequence of allowing the Syrian and Russian forces to reorganise: by mid 2019, three of the four 'de-escalation zones' had been taken over by the Syrian government. The process changed the dynamics of the conflict and enabled the military victory of the Syrian government.

That strategy, which repositioned Russia as a power to be reckoned with, put the final nail in the coffin of Pax Americana and heralded the emergence of a multipolar world in which the space for mediation was modified. Previously, the liberal world under American hegemony had been conducive to mediation because it imposed a hierarchy of power and encouraged the belligerents to conform to it; now, local, regional and international rivalries with competing interests made it more difficult to negotiate any reduction in violence, much less a peace agreement. This new order prompted the resignation of Mouin Rabbani, Principal Political Affairs Officer in de Mistura's mediation effort, with Rabbani judging that 'the United Nations [had] become part of the problem [... p]romoting the illusion of purposeful mediation'[11] when this was no longer the case—if it ever had been. It was during this period that 'the war of sieges' was at its worst.

The war of sieges: were the ICRC and the UN complicit in war crimes?

The 'war of sieges' in Syria began in 2012 and grew increasingly intense until 2019, when the government of President Assad had recaptured most of the territory. At that point the conflict became a low-intensity war; before that, towns and villages had been surrounded, subjected to a deluge of bombs and deprived of humanitarian aid for months. The Syrian army didn't have enough fighters to take towns in street battles when every house might be booby-trapped, hence the use of a strategy as Machiavellian as it was ruthless: its tactics involved encircling the towns held by the opposition (who employed the same tactics on a few occasions themselves) followed by 'the routine denial of delivery of vital foodstuffs, health items and other essential supplies to besieged enclaves, as well as indiscriminate attacks and deliberate attacks targeting civilian infrastructure, including hospitals, in order to erode the viability of life under the control of opposing sides'.[12] This is the strategy the Independent International Commission of Inquiry charmingly referred to as 'starve or surrender'.[13]

In an earlier report, the International Commission noted that 'over 600,000 Syrian men, women and children countrywide remain trapped in besieged locations'.[14] Humanitarian aid, which was part and parcel of the government's military strategy to control the situation, was denounced by humanitarian organisations, which nevertheless hoped aid would somehow 'trickle down' to the besieged cities. The regime used their control of aid to starve the population in rebel-held towns, subjecting them also to indiscriminate shelling and using prohibited weapons, including chemical weapons and cluster munitions, beating them down until, with cruel irony and deliberate perversity, it offered them 'reconciliation agreements'. These were more 'surrender agreements', but Damascus wanted to maintain the fiction of a reconciled people, in a compliment that vice paid to virtue. It set up 'reconciliation committees' made up of

Syrian security agents, local dignitaries and opposition militia leaders, who would sometimes negotiate the terms of the agreements by WhatsApp or Viber messaging. The agreements also involved one or several intermediaries—Iranian, Qatari, even Turkish diplomats, the Centre for Humanitarian Dialogue, a Russian commander—depending on the local configuration and power relations. Sadly, the terms, often vague, heightened the risk of divergent (mis)interpretations, forcing the intermediaries to ask themselves if what they were doing was an acceptable compromise (if it served to alleviate people's suffering) or if it were a form of complicity that helped the regime to send the populations it deemed hostile to peripheral areas. The matter was hotly debated and everyone had their own assessment of the lines not to be crossed.

Yet with few exceptions, these agreements provided for the departure of combatants and populations, the exchange of prisoners or human remains, and the release of detainees. The United Nations was usually not involved, the Syrian authorities wanting to keep themselves at arm's length from these unorthodox deals, but it was often notified as soon as an agreement was reached and, at the request of the fleeing populations, would dispatch a couple of armoured vehicles to ensure that the evacuation convoy was not shot at and could reach its destination; nevertheless, the mere presence of these peripheral escorts worked to the advantage of Damascus, which used them to claim international legitimacy. Thus, between 2012 and 2018, hundreds of thousands of men, women and children were 'cleansed' through humanitarian corridors, which were in fact routes of expulsion in a policy of 'demographic engineering', to use the Council of Europe's term.[15]

And as the Syrian government started to regain the upper hand, the terms of these local deals grew even more opaque, more like marching orders than agreements. The International Commission pointed out: 'Overall, the evacuations taking place across the country appear to be aimed at altering the political demographics of previously besieged enclaves, redrawing and consolidating the bases of political support.'[16] People knew that when they left they would lose everything; that they were in fact forcibly abandoning their homes and possessions. As for those who remained, their fate was in the hands of the pro-regime forces.

One of the worst examples of this system was in Aleppo, the city de Mistura had dreamed of making a haven of stability, even peace. The siege started on 10 July 2012, and intensified until 2016, when it was focused on the eastern part of the city held by the opposition Free Syrian Army and other largely Sunni groups, such as the Levant Front and the al-Qaeda-affiliated al-Nusra Front. The fighting resulted in widespread devastation, prompting combatants to refer to it as the 'mother of all battles' or 'Syria's Stalingrad'. A UN report[17] listed multiple violations of the law of war, among them indiscriminate bombardments by the Russian air force and Syrian artillery; the use of chemical weapons by government forces; the shelling of hospitals, schools and civilian populations; and the use of starvation as a weapon of war. Finally, on 14 December 2016, under a confidentially mediated ceasefire and evacuation agreement, some 35,000 men, women and children left Aleppo under ICRC auspices for the opposition-held, Islamist bastion of Idlib, thirty-five miles away in northwest Syria—but not before some 31,000 people had died in one of the longest sieges in modern history. According to the International Commission, 'As warring parties agreed to the evacuation of eastern Aleppo for strategic reasons—and not for the security of civilians or imperative military necessity, which permit the displacement of thousands—the Aleppo evacuation agreement amounts to the war crime of forced displacement'.[18] This was a serious accusation for the intermediaries that had organised the agreement, for the ICRC, whose delegates supervised the evacuation, and for the UN, which was also present.

Such accusations are easier to make with the benefit of hindsight, like a game of chess where all the moves are analysed after the fact. They do not take into account the volatility of the situation and the difficulty of positioning oneself in real time. What options did the ICRC and the UN have at the time, if not to submit to a higher moral obligation: to save lives? That, in any case, is what the ICRC's spokesperson, Iolanda Jaquemet, said: 'The evacuations helped avert an even greater humanitarian disaster in Aleppo ... when people who played no part in the violence were trapped and had literally no place to run.'[19]

In eastern Ghouta, the siege lasted for more than five years, from 2013 to 2018. The population was exhausted, victim not only of shelling and hunger, but also of sarin gas. Casualties increased, yet there was no solution in sight. They had to flee, but how? In April 2018, three deals were finally struck with the help of the Centre for Humanitarian Dialogue. Over 100,000 people were evacuated to Idlib, where they found themselves once more on the front lines—and where many remain. The evacuation sparked fierce debate within the small world of the mediation community: should they have facilitated a policy of population 'cleansing', in violation of the law of war? One of the mediators involved in the evacuation agreements—wishing to remain anonymous—expressed ambivalence and discomfort at having taken part in the negotiations:

> These agreements bought the population a measure of respite for a few weeks at best, without achieving anything but to push people towards the Idlib funnel. We facilitated the mass exodus of hundreds of thousands of people from eastern Ghouta, Homs, Aleppo, Wadi Barada and southern Syria only to create an open-air

prison in Idlib for 3 million people who faced a choice between being bombed or going into exile in Turkey.

In his address on receiving the Carnegie Wateler Peace Prize on 3 November 2022 on behalf of the Centre for Humanitarian Dialogue, Executive Director David Harland considered the choices his organisation had made in Syria, drawing on the lessons of Srebrenica twenty-five years after that tragedy in Bosnia-Herzegovina:

> Was our work helping the Syrian regime to complete a job that was fundamentally wrong? Could we, like UNHCR in Srebrenica a quarter of a century before, be accused of legitimating or even enabling a huge crime? Looking back, I have tried to understand that conundrum, wherever it arises, in terms of the primacy of the right to life. However much we may wish it weren't so, there is a hierarchy of rights. At least at desperate moments, rights do get traded off, one against others. Because, at any given moment, the right to life surely trumps the others. Some rights can still have some meaning if deferred, including justice, but the right to life cannot be deferred, and can't be parsed.[20]

Bottom-up pacification turned out to be a chimera. In an internationalised war in which there was not the least common denominator between the local, regional and international parties, mediation played a secondary role. It adapted to shifts in the balance of power and was left with little choice but to look on as Russian support of Syria led to military victory by the regime. Local ceasefires and evacuation agreements, sometimes overseen by the UN and the ICRC, saved lives but set out no political vision.

The question remains unanswered: is the UN right to persist with its mediation efforts in such circumstances? Its raison d'être is 'to avoid the scourge of war' and to mediate an end to conflict. That's part of its DNA. Did its presence serve to limit people's suffering by facilitating the delivery of humanitarian aid and organising ceasefires that proved to be fragile? No doubt, yes. But the opposite could just as easily be argued: isn't persisting with a failing mediation effort serving as an alibi tantamount to living in a parallel universe? Would it not have been better, as it had for Sadako Ogata in Bosnia in 1993, to withdraw and bring the parties face to face with their responsibilities? If so, the illusion of a genuine mediation effort would have been dispelled; however, given the cruelty of the regime, the situation would probably have been even worse.

Syria demonstrated that a government can inflict carnage on its population with impunity, a harbinger of the war in Ukraine, where the question of respecting standards for the protection of civilians is also moot. Today, Syria has been destroyed and 90 per cent of the population lives below the poverty line, the UN mediation effort continues, yet after a decade of war and peace talks, there is no political solution in sight.

10

THE SAHEL

TALKING WITH JIHADISTS

In the first part of this book, I looked at how anti-terrorist norms excluded from mediation those perceived as 'enemies of humankind', then at how official mediators were themselves banned from talking with 'terrorist organisations'. In this second part, I have looked at how mediators have tried—not always successfully—to walk a narrow line and stay on the right side of the force for good. What I would also like to highlight is how the 'straitjacket' of security considerations came to hold sway in the Sahel, a vast region covering Mali, northern Burkina Faso, Niger, Chad, parts of northern Cameroon, Nigeria, the Central African Republic, South Sudan, Eritrea and Ethiopia.

Just as it took nearly twenty years for the United States to admit that the ideological prism of the war on terror through which it viewed the Taliban was not productive, Europe has for too long been blinded by security considerations on its southern flank. The ideology of counterterrorism has for years supplanted analysis of the political and social realities of Sahelian societies, serving only to exacerbate the jihadist violence that started in northern Mali in 2012 and is now spreading to the countries of the Gulf of Guinea.

Let us start with the context. The NATO intervention in Libya in March 2011 had a profound impact on events in Syria, but even more in the Sahel, prompting the Tuareg, a large Berber ethnic group of traditionally nomadic pastoralists who had been serving in the Libyan army, to return to their countries of origin there to boost the numbers of existing armed groups.

In early 2012, a fresh Tuareg rebellion broke out in northern Mali. Historical misunderstandings and mutual distrust between those in the capital, Bamako, and those in the north of the country had been a major factor of Malian instability for decades. By ignoring northern aspirations for economic development and political representation, the Malian authorities paved the way for violent contestation and separatist action. From independence in 1960 to 2011, there were three Tuareg rebellions[1] and ineffective north–south peace agreements. The ethnic divisions and lawlessness that arose in the aftermath of each rebellion and the Malian state's withdrawal presented a window of opportunity for armed groups to settle in the north. Mixing with local populations, these groups managed gradually to gain influence before the 2012 crisis, demanding the independence of 'Azawad', the northern half of Mali.

A fourth Tuareg rebellion in 2012 was swiftly marginalised by the jihadist Tuareg group Ansar Dine (Defenders of the Faith), led by the charismatic Iyad ag Ghali.[2] Together with the Movement for Unity and Jihad in West Africa (MUJAO), a militant Islamist organisation that had broken with Al-Qaeda in the Islamic Maghreb, Ansar Dine seized the north of Mali and, in January 2013, turned south and appeared poised to take Bamako. French forces, acting at the request of the Malian authorities installed in the capital as a result of the March 2012 coup, launched Operation Serval in January 2013 and Operation Barkhane in August 2014, initially repelling the attackers. At the instigation of France, in February 2013 the UN Security Council, the United States and the European Union added to their lists organisations and individuals considered 'terrorist' and affiliated with al-Qaeda, in particular Iyad ag Ghali and MUJAO. France then opted for a policy that it upheld until relations with Mali deteriorated in early 2022, when the new junta demanded that France and the Europeans withdraw their forces.

The policy had been initiated in 2013 by President François Hollande and was renewed by Emmanuel Macron, who, in an interview with the weekly *Jeune Afrique*, kept to the path of his predecessors and to the official line of the European Union and the United

States in portraying his approach as a merciless struggle: 'We don't talk to terrorists. We fight them.'[3] Since the beginning of the armed rebellion in Mali in 2012, fear that a Taliban-inspired 'Sahelistan' would emerge on Europe's southern flank had conditioned strategy, which was to eradicate jihadist groups and provide unwavering support for the government in Bamako, even though it was perceived as corrupt and illegitimate in the country's remoter regions, unable as it was to provide security and basic services such as education and health. These were two serious mistakes for which successive French governments would ultimately pay a high price.

A turning point in the conflict was the 2015 Agreement for Peace and Reconciliation.[4] The Malian government, a coalition of pro-government armed groups from northern Mali called the Platform and the Coordination of Azawad Movements (Coordination des mouvements de l'Azawad, CMA)—an alliance of rebel groups—convened in Bamako and signed an agreement to restore peace. The signatories were under great pressure from an international mediation team to accept the final text, which was drafted after less than a year of often indirect negotiations. The mediation team was led by Algeria and comprised representatives of the United Nations Multidimensional Integrated Stabilization Mission in Mali (MINUSMA), the Economic Community of West African States (ECOWAS), the African Union and the European Union, as well as the United States and France, who were initially designated 'friends of the mediation'.[5] The agreement sought to restore peace in Mali principally through a process of decentralisation or regionalisation, reconstituting a national army from the members of the former armed groups that were signatories, and to boost the economy (particularly in the north), based on dialogue, justice and national reconciliation.

The belligerents, who signed the agreement reluctantly, never respected it; however, the powerful mediators decided to 'make peace' between the Malian government, its allies and the CMA. The jihadist groups listed as 'terrorist' were excluded: by the terms of the UN Security Council resolution 1373, 'terrorist' groups cannot be part of any negotiations. This was the core principle of the 'war on terror' that I described earlier and which aimed to isolate and then eradicate 'terrorists'.

The mechanical application of abstract anti-terrorism rules made little sense. In the case at hand, the United Nations and Western governments distinguished between 'terrorists' (who were thus excluded from the negotiations) and 'insurgents' using violence to legitimate ends and participating in peace negotiations. However, they all used violence, and the armed groups to which they belonged were not mutually exclusive. Moreover, as the scholar and Sahel specialist Ferdaous Bouhlel wrote, 'Not only is Ansar Dine rooted in the community and an offshoot of long-standing Tuareg demands for the independence of Azawad, it also professes a Salafist ideology.'[6]

In the most obvious result, Ansar Dine, which had previously had a national agenda but now espoused—albeit in words only—the cause of a globalised jihad, was further radicalised and marginalised.

Western governments, who had put all their eggs in the security basket, were unyielding in their support for a Malian state that had nevertheless lost its legitimacy in the eyes of part of its population. The more the violence spread—in the north, to the centre and finally to the south—the more France and its allies hoped to win militarily against the 'terrorists' and to reform the state's governance. They would lose on both counts.

The cycle of violence

Western governments supported, in theory, an 'integrated approach' that included development and set out with this aim in mind; however, no one ever saw the fruit of the costly projects they launched. As for reform of the state, it was too complicated and too politically sensitive to implement, especially since the state was already in decline. In fact, the more the situation deteriorated in Mali, the more priority was attached to counterterrorism rather than mediation or dialogue with armed groups.

The intervention in 2013 of 13,000 UN peace-keepers backed by the armed forces of France and the United States, other European countries and the G5 Sahel countries (Burkina Faso, Chad, Mali, Mauritania and Niger) failed to restore security. By law, the state was sovereign, yet on the ground it was contested by dozens of armed groups. Moreover, the violence of the jihadist groups was compounded by inter-community clashes between sedentary farmers and semi-nomadic herders throughout the Sahel, where the population was growing more rapidly than anywhere else in the world (women have on average six to seven children), further intensifying competition for scarce resources; at the same time, albeit to a lesser extent, climate change did away with the long-established transhumance corridors negotiated between herders and farming communities. The herders encroached on agricultural land, sparking fresh conflicts with the communities with which they competed for increasingly scarce resources.

The jihadist groups exploited the inter-community tensions while the state was absent or, worse, took sides and armed one community against the other, prompting the creation of self-defence militias. Many Fulani, a large nomadic group of traditional herders, considering themselves stigmatised, joined the jihadist ranks, further exacerbating the violence.

The French presence, initially perceived as a force for liberation, soon came to be seen by the population as an occupier. Undeterred, France was even more determined to eradicate terrorism following a wave of deadly attacks on French soil: on 9 January 2015, at the kosher supermarket Hyper-Cacher and the office of the satirical weekly *Charlie-Hebdo*; on 13 November at the Bataclan and the Stade de France (claiming 131 lives); and on 14 July 2016, in Nice, where 86 people were killed and over 400 wounded. Paris conducted its 'Sahelian Policy' through the prism of its fight against terrorism and put pressure on the governments of Mali, Niger and Burkina Faso to follow suit.

Then, on 1 March 2017, four groups affiliated with al-Qaeda united to form a new movement known by its acronym in Arabic, JNIM (Jama'at el nusra wa al-islam wa el muslimin, or Support Group for Islam and Muslims). Headed by Iyad ag Ghali, their attacks grew increasingly deadly. Alarmed by the deteriorating situation, a group of regional experts writing in *Le Monde* affirmed that 'the French military tool must be subordinated to a realistic political project defined by Sahelian societies'.[7] They explained that jihadist groups represented a segment of the population frustrated by the intransigent state of affairs: 'France's refusal to engage in dialogue with so-called jihadist groups flies in the face of reality on the ground. France runs the risk of ending up on the wrong side of history if it continues to refuse to budge'.[8] Their cry of alarm fell on deaf ears. Paris and, in its wake, Western governments made the strategic choice to support the states of the Sahel against the risk of a globalised jihad.

The primary victims of that choice were the people, caught between the binary logic of both counterterrorism and the jihadists. As Ferdaous Bouhlel wrote: 'The imposition of a polarising approach based on suspicion and the need for the population to distance itself from the jihadists had a counterproductive effect: it neutralised a whole range of local regulatory mechanisms, to the detriment of a possible transformation of the violence.'[9] The people were most often only aware of the state by its absence or by the occasional presence of military forces and pro-government militias that committed abuses and only served to escalate the conflict.

Iyad ag Ghali heaped scorn on the broken promises of governments and the international community: 'They promised security and development and construction. Where is their security, their stability, their development and their construction, in view of what our oppressed people are undergoing: the misfortunes of bombardments, destruction and intrusions into homes?'[10]

In addition, the populations in remote areas found it difficult to identify with the central authorities that emerged from French colonisation, which imposed a highly centralised vision of power and a secular, democratic constitution. Hence the growing gap between them and a state perceived as the expression of a neo-colonial bureaucracy, often characterised by poor governance and corruption, and appearing to deny their cultural identity and the central place of Islam in it. This did not mean, however, that they were necessarily enchanted by the jihadist groups professing an ultra-conservative religiosity. Understanding this, the jihadists used a mix of seduction and intimidation; to gain acceptance and not alienate the population, they tended to adopt a pragmatic attitude, allowing communities a degree of autonomy while restoring security by eliminating the criminal gangs involved in cattle rustling and extortion.

In light of this, the failure of the international community's anti-terrorist policy has since been acknowledged. It radicalised positions and accelerated the destabilisation of the Sahel, allowing the jihadist groups to expand towards the Gulf of Guinea. And the carnage continues: in 2021, armed groups carried out more than 800 deadly attacks, uprooted some 450,000 people in Mali, Niger and Burkina Faso, and forced tens of thousands more to flee to neighbouring countries. In Burkina Faso alone, nearly two million people have been displaced internally. In 2022, 5,700 schools were closed because of the security situation, depriving more than one million students of education.[11]

To talk or not to talk?

As the security situation in the Sahel deteriorated, the positions of the region's leaders began to shift, even as Paris refused to budge. In 2017 and 2019, the National Agreement Conference and the Inclusive National Dialogue in Mali, sponsored by the government and attended by officials, politicians, representatives of religious organisations, traditional authorities and civil society agencies, recommended that talks be started with the jihadist leaders. A very short-lived attempt took place in July 2017, when Mali's Prime Minister Abdoulaye Idrissa Maïga asked a senior Muslim figure to whom he was close, Imam Mahmoud Dicko, to carry out a 'mission of good offices'[12] to jihadist groups in central Mali; however, a few months later, apparently under French pressure, President Ibrahim Boubacar Keïta opposed the move, aborting one of the rare attempts at dialogue between the government in Bamako and the jihadist groups.

Clashes between communities multiplied, first in the centre of Mali, then in Niger and Burkina Faso, thus forcing the issue of the need for local dialogue and, yet again, raising the dilemma—to talk or not to talk, illustrating also the ambiguity of European countries. They finance peace talks with communities and armed groups, some of which have links with 'terrorist organisations'; therefore, would dialogue and its outcome be tantamount to collusion between the mediators and the belligerents? Would engaging in dialogue with 'terrorist organisations' start Europe on the path towards acknowledging their legitimacy? Would the search for an illusory peace lead to populations being sacrificed and constitute a step towards complicity? Conversely, did it still make sense to refuse to explore avenues for dialogue when any military solution was out of reach?

And so it was that a first discreet, almost covert, shift took place: in 2018 Prime Minister Maïga asked the Centre for Humanitarian Dialogue to mediate in central Mali—but not with blacklisted Islamist insurgents. The three Sahelian states most affected (Mali, Burkina Faso and Niger) and the European states involved carefully outsourced 'grassroots' processes of talks between the various parties (armed groups, communities, self-defence militias and so on) to a few local and international private mediation organisations (the Centre for Humanitarian Dialogue, Search for Common Ground, Promediation). The aim was to de-escalate and then prevent fighting, restore harmony through inter-community agreements, and identify and resolve the causes of the conflict, which were often rooted in access to resources.

The Centre for Humanitarian Dialogue facilitated the mediation of more than fifty local agreements in Mali, Niger and Burkina Faso in which armed jihadist groups were indirectly involved.[13] The agreements covered the return of displaced persons, access to wells and resources in general, transhumance corridors, the management of grazing land, the return of stolen livestock, conflict prevention, methods of justice and reparation, and forgiveness 'for all past acts'. They were limited geographically, for example between the Dogon and the Fulani in Koro Cercle; between the Idourfan and Ibogolitan communities of the Gao and Ménaka regions of Mali and Tillabéry in Niger; or between the Fulani and Arab Mahamid communities of Foulatari, N'guelbeli, Goudoumaria and Mainé Soroa municipalities in Niger's Diffa region.[14] The talks, conducted by local mediators (employed by a private Western organisation), represented the continuation of a long-standing Sahelian tradition of negotiation and dialogue between communities in what were historically weak states.

In the Sahel, local agreements like these act as a balm. They are light years removed from the process of 'imposing' peace vaunted by Boutros Boutros-Ghali in the 1992 *Agenda for Peace*, which justified UN military involvement without the consent of both parties to safeguard international security. The local agreements reflect reality on the ground, where, in the face of a failing state and heightened community tensions, mediators struggle with their counterparts to make life easier for people in limited areas. They represent the art of the possible, even if without the means or ambition to tackle the root causes of the problem, chiefly the absence of basic state services, poor governance and centralised institutions inherited from the French colonialists. These new processes are fragile, at the mercy of a change in the balance of power or the emergence of new armed groups, but they allow for at least a temporary return to calm. More deeply, they testify to the need to find pragmatic and adaptive solutions that take into account local conditions and respect local culture.

The call for dialogue with 'terrorist organisations'

After years of failed counterterrorism action, the voice of pragmatism started to make itself heard in Malian society, calling for dialogue with the jihadists. In February 2020, breaking with the security policy he had spearheaded since 2013, Malian President Keïta said that he was ready to talk with insurgents: 'Talking with the jihadists and fighting terrorism is not a contradiction. I have the duty and the mission today to create all possible spaces and do everything in my power so that, one way or another, we can achieve whatever can reduce the violence. The time has come to explore certain avenues.'[15]

This yielded results. In July 2020, a first agreement was concluded in the Koro area between Dogon communities and a jihadist group. Rather than written, this was a verbal declaration of honour on a few points concerning, above all, the application of Sharia principles. In April 2021, an agreement facilitated by the High Islamic Council led to a ceasefire in the village of Farabougou,[16] the application of Sharia law and acceptance of the population's neutrality in the war between jihadist groups and the Malian army. In exchange, both the Fulani and Bambara populations could resume their respective activities. The agreement, albeit geographically very limited, reflected a change in approach.

In Burkina Faso, despite the government's stated refusal to negotiate with 'terrorists', secret high-level talks were held between representatives of the authorities and leaders of the al-Qaeda-affiliated JNIM in 2020.[17] They resulted in a short-lived ceasefire and the release of members of armed groups, but the dialogue did not go further. And in a kind of domino effect, in late 2020 Niger's President Mohamed Bazoum announced talks with the jihadist leaders of the Islamic State in the Greater Sahara, as a result of which several jihadist prisoners were released and received at the presidential palace. This policy of outreach also took the form of emissaries to other jihadist leaders, to 'help lighten the burden under which our soldiers labour'.[18]

First talks with al-Qaeda

With these talks unfolding in the background, unofficial whispers began to circulate in EU circles in Brussels and in Germany about the possibility of engaging with the JNIM. The whispers stressed the difference between the radicalism of Islamic State, which made negotiations unlikely, and the JNIM, which represented a socio-political reality and which, experience had shown, respected local agreements; however, and in the face of cautiously growing support for the idea, this was a pragmatic position that Paris did not share. In December 2021, the International Crisis Group, an influential conflict-prevention organisation, issued a report entitled *Mali: Enabling Dialogue with the Jihadist Coalition*

JNIM,[19] which followed a 2019 report entitled *Speaking with the 'Bad Guys': Toward Dialogue with Central Mali's Jihadists*.[20] Even the UN Secretary-General, António Guterres, changed his tune: 'There will be groups with which we can talk, and which will have an interest in engaging in this dialogue to become political actors in the future.' He excluded those affiliated with the Islamic State, because their 'terrorist radicalism is such that there will be nothing to be done with them'.[21] Smaïl Chergui, former African Union Commissioner for Peace and Security, was also open to talking with the jihadists.[22] The times sure were changing.

The JNIM, unlike the Islamic State, with which it was openly at war, hailed developments in Afghanistan, marked by the Doha Agreement between the Taliban and the United States, as a major victory. Gone were the times when it would assert that, 'You don't bargain about God'. The Doha Agreement set a precedent and the JNIM let it be known that it was open to dialogue, posing as a precondition the departure of foreign troops.

Since President Keïta's bold declarations, two successive military juntas have seized power in Bamako, in 2020 and 2021; then the Kremlin-affiliated Wagner Group deployed several hundred mercenaries to Mali, while the new authorities demanded that French and European troops leave the country before talks had even begun.

Today, in the climate of the new cold war, the African continent is becoming a pitch on which Russia, China and Western countries play out their rivalries. Jihadist insurgencies now affect Togo, Benin and Côte d'Ivoire, and the populations living in peripheral areas are caught in a vice between government troops and jihadist groups carrying out indiscriminate attacks against communities accused of colluding with the enemy.

The case is clear: in the Sahel, reality has laid waste to the 'security first' considerations imposed by the ideology of the 'war on terror'. Mediation and dialogue at local level have never been more essential. They provide an ad hoc, limited response, help to avoid an even more deadly cycle of violence, and open a broader question: would more ambitious mediation efforts relating to the model of society be conceivable? On what values should co-habitation be predicated? The Sahel is currently torn between several models of society: the autocratic model of General Sissi's Egypt; the secular and democratic model inherited from colonisation; and the theocratic model. Can these co-exist and peacefully share the same spaces in urban and rural areas? If so, what are the benefits, but also the risks, for the populations concerned? These are all questions that both local and international mediators must consider to avoid doing more harm than good in their efforts to assist the parties.

In the Sahel, the fight against terrorism, in the ideological forms it has taken, has been a terrible waste. By disregarding reality, France and its allies repeated the mistakes of American policy, which itself wanted to act free of Afghan reality. Without indulging in romanticism, and without denying the real difficulties and dangers, I believe the return to peace and security of Sahelian societies can only be achieved through dialogue and the development of a model for co-habiting. It is up to these societies to develop those models, adapting them to the particular needs, aspirations and sensibilities of their diverse populations.

CONCLUSION

THE DEREGULATION OF FORCE

In the space of three decades, mediators have seen their field of action transformed. We have gone from soft to hard power, from 'peace dividends' to the return of war in Europe, from the end of one cold war to a new one involving the confrontation between the West and Russia, even China, from the unipolar world of Pax Americana hegemony to a multipolar world, from the dream of an all-powerful United Nations to the organisation's marginalisation.

The most striking moment in this epochal shift occurred on 27 April 2022, when UN Secretary-General António Guterres was in the Kremlin with President Vladimir Putin, trying to arrange UN-facilitated mediation between Ukraine and Russia. Moscow declined the offer, with a dramatic response the following day, while Guterres was in Kyiv. The Ukrainian capital, which had been given a reprieve from bombing for a fortnight, was again struck by two Russian missiles just as Guterres emerged from a meeting with President Volodymyr

Zelensky.[1] These missiles were the reply of the Russian head of state: a brutal *nyet* to the UN Secretary-General's mediation proposal. Never before had the United Nations been slapped in the face so publicly by a major power, its haplessness exposed, confirming fears that its time had come and gone, that it was now doomed to the same fate as the defunct League of Nations, which failed to create an effective system of collective security after the First World War.

UN-sponsored mediation boomed in the 1990s, in part supported by a global hierarchy of power topped by the US. American might and influence was a leveraged guarantor of stability and respect for the peace agreements most often negotiated and concluded by the UN. American hegemony was thus able to affirm its liberal standards, even if democracy, the rule of law and human rights were slow to materialise in countries in transition. And though the emergence of an international justice system—the International Criminal Court—complicated the work of mediators by potentially indicting political or military leaders, thus preventing them from participating in peace negotiations, this was not a crippling obstacle. Despite the fact that international justice was and continues to be used for political ends, it has had the merit of creating an ecosystem intended to fight impunity.

The attacks of 11 September 2001, the launch of the 'war on terror' and American-led military interventions in Kosovo, Iraq and Libya undermined the liberal international order. Ostensibly launched to export democracy and stability, they instead brought greater chaos and misery to the Middle East and Central Asia, and drastically reduced the space for authorised official mediation efforts. In the so-called 'just war' on 'terror', the lists of 'pariah organisations' grew steadily longer and certain governments seized on the ideological moment to throw off the shackles of international law, citing the need to fight an enemy that had to be eliminated. Military operations paved the way for the deregulation of force, to the benefit of authoritarian regimes. The February 2022 attack on Ukraine by Russia, for the warped purpose of fighting 'Nazism', is the most extreme example. Earlier, the Myanmar regime had carried out a systematic campaign of persecution and 'ethnic cleansing' against the Rohingya. The campaign culminated in 2017, but the ensuing condemnation had very little impact.

With the end of Pax Americana, an era is drawing to a close. The return of geostrategic competition with Russia, the American debacle in Afghanistan in August 2021 (despite two trillion dollars spent over twenty years), followed by the withdrawal of American forces from Iraq, the slow but constant rise of China, war in the Middle East and North Africa (Syria, Yemen, Libya, Israel-Palestine)—all have upset the international equation and threaten American hegemony. So has the growing assertiveness of regional powers such as India, Turkey,

Pakistan, Iran, South Africa, Brazil and others on the international scene. They are liberating themselves from their former 'sponsors', while the world's economic centre of gravity is shifting from Europe to Asia.

The challenges to mediation

The result is a series of daunting challenges for mediation, which in the space of three decades has been transformed by various factors, including the multiplication of parties to internal conflicts. Now, dozens and sometimes hundreds of armed groups with divergent interests struggle to gain the upper hand. In the eastern part of the Democratic Republic of the Congo, for example, various militias, security forces and a plethora of foreign entities are in conflict, rendering the process of mediation much more complex. I wrote about this in the chapter on Syria: in that internationalised civil war, the hostilities between local entities were constantly whetted by the many external participants, each pursuing its own agenda and whittling away at the space for mediation.

This mounting complexity obliges mediators to work as closely as possible with the various players in conflict zones, while engaging in diplomatic efforts with the external powers involved. The mediators' task is rendered all the more difficult by the deals concluded between these external powers to ensure that they do not enter into direct conflict with each other while the war is being waged. This is the paradoxical situation that has now arisen in Syria and is emblematic of a hitherto unprecedented development: Russia has signed separate military agreements with, respectively, the United States, Israel and Turkey to avoid a direct confrontation. Thus, to the internationalised civil war in Syria is added the Iranian–Israeli confrontation in the face of which Russia has retreated to the background. Israel can therefore strike Iranian targets in Syria without fear of action by the Russian air force and anti-aircraft defence systems. These deals, purely transactional, are based on volatile alliances that reconfigure themselves according to the shifting interests of political players and particular themes. In today's planet-wide Great Game, Saudi Arabia and Russia might establish a one-off alliance; communist China rush to normalise relations with the theocratic regime of the Taliban; the United States devise the 2020 Abraham Accords (purporting to establish peace between Israel, the United Arab Emirates and Bahrain but in reality aimed at forging an alliance against the Iran of the mullahs); and so on. These deals reflect a logic of power and often even a logic of war, and not the search for peace on which mediation is predicated. They are genuine manifestations of *realpolitik* that nevertheless shape the environment in which mediation takes place.

Even when countries are in conflict, they can conclude ad hoc agreements for purely transactional purposes that don't bring them an inch closer to peace. For example, thanks to American mediation, Israel and Lebanon agreed on the maritime border between them even though they are technically at war[2] and while Hezbollah—Lebanon's strongest political-military force—remains a 'terrorist organisation' in the eyes of Israel (and Western governments). By the same token, mediation by Turkey and the United Nations has led to the conclusion[3] and even the renewal[4] of an agreement between Russia and Ukraine on their exports of grain and fertiliser, thus avoiding famine in certain African countries while the war between Ukrainian and Russian forces continues to rage.

The emergence of this deeply divided multipolar world poses a huge challenge for mediators. The definition of common values and standards has become a bone of contention between the Western countries, Russia, China and the diverse members of the Global South, and between different models of society—liberal, authoritarian, theocratic and their many hybrids—that are themselves riddled with contradictions and tension. Human rights, the responsibility to protect and international justice are the subject of harsh ideological clashes between their promoters and those who, like Russia and China, see them as instruments of Western interference. On the battlefield, this confrontation results in conventional armies that ignore the minimum standards established by the law of war, such as the duty to protect civilians. Is the very idea of an international 'community' still relevant when standards are eroded to such an extent?

In his *Prison Notebooks*, Italian philosopher Antonio Gramsci[5] warned: 'The old world is dying, and the new world struggles to be born: this interregnum is the time of monsters.' What role can mediators play when even minimum standards are flouted? Does their symbolic power and moral authority still carry weight with the belligerents? At what point do they become complicit in policies of 'ethnic cleansing' or 'demographic engineering'? In these pages I have set out the ethical dilemmas that arose during the Second World War, in Bosnia-Herzegovina, Syria and the Sahel, aiming to show the difficulties mediators face when trying to gauge the exact moment when their work might be responsible for causing harm, rather than helping. In today's even more polarised and fractured geopolitical context, that assessment is even harder to make. Hence the need to set up internal procedures for efficient deliberation within mediation teams, mechanisms by which they call themselves into question, discuss divergent points of view and thus limit the risk that they will endorse, even support, those for whom the existence of a peace process simply allows them to better pursue their criminal policies. This is essential work that limits the risk of an otherwise imperceptible slide towards complicity. It ensures that the action undertaken remains in line with the ethics of mediation.

The second challenge to negotiation relates to the limitations imposed by counterterrorism legislation and the straitjacket of the mindset behind the restrictions related to the 'war on terror'. Blind to local realities, counterterrorism continues to stymie mediation efforts of the United Nations and states from reaching out to proscribed armed groups, further radicalising them as a result.

To circumvent this, certain African governments have adopted a pragmatic attitude and mandated mediation NGOs to explore other avenues of dialogue with those who have been officially outlawed. The first results of that approach can be seen in the Sahel, where moderately successful dialogue with jihadist groups became a rebuttal to the failure of the 'war on terror' to elicit peace, inspiring other African governments to do the same or similar; however, the path to a negotiated settlement is never without complications and risks, including the possibility of legitimising armed groups that won't renounce their oppressive agenda. There is also a risk to local mediators, who often find themselves caught in the crossfire of the conflict they are hoping to resolve. These mediators, on whom the private mediation organisations rely, will be themselves immersed in the reality of war, as will their families. They are frequently intimidated and threatened by the belligerents, suspected of being traitors by some and spies by others. Their impartiality is constantly called into doubt. Many have paid with their lives for their commitment to peace in their countries. Despite the risks, openness to dialogue frees the parties from the chains of the international obligations set by the fight against terrorism—context wins out over the ideology of the 'war on terror', as it did when the Colombian government reached an agreement with the FARC at a time when the FARC was on the list of terrorist organisations to be shunned.

The third challenge facing mediators today is the emergence of 'post-truth'. Fake news and propaganda are as old as war, but the power of the internet and social networks has notably boosted the capacity for harm in this context of polarisation and fragmentation. Mediation involves exchange, the confrontation of ideas, negotiation. However, if the material facts are themselves contested at the most elementary level, if lying becomes a state policy, if the absolute relativism of 'alternative truths' dominates in the globalised space, the capacity to live together but also to negotiate on common terms will hit a wall. In the case of the Russian–Ukrainian conflict, the outlook for mediation is all the more complicated in that it is disrupted by the public airing given to the Orwellian propaganda of the Kremlin when it asserts, for example, that the videos and photos of bodies from the Kyiv suburb of Bucha are part of 'an elaborate hoax'.[6] Interestingly, there have been some new mediation efforts, for instance in Bosnia-Herzegovina, to limit hate speech, harassment, disinformation and the use of bots and trolls on social media during the election period,[7] but the challenge is enormous.

Global security

State security is now also related to global security, as we have experienced in recent years: dealing with pandemics, rapid climate change, fake news or organised crime networks exceeds the capacity of individual states and increasingly requires cross-border cooperation and communication. The Covid-19 pandemic saw a rise in national selfishness but also, belatedly, the establishment of solidarity mechanisms. On 23 May 2020, the UN Secretary-General called for a Covid-19-related 'global ceasefire',[8] opening doors to mediation that led to truces between belligerents in Colombia, Sudan and the Central African Republic, in turn allowing coordinated efforts to vaccinate local populations against the coronavirus.[9] Elsewhere, talks have facilitated commitments by parties to limit hate speech on social media in countries in conflict and to prevent peace processes from being torpedoed by public disinformation campaigns.[10] Some states and mediation NGOs are now grappling with the merits of negotiating with powerful criminal cartels,[11] although here, too, the intervention of third parties must be based on ethical rules.

Unlike the Cold War era and the years that followed, the world today is infinitely more interdependent and connected. The butterfly effect is being felt in human affairs: the war in Ukraine has reminded us that the fate of millions of Africans depends on deliveries of wheat from a European region at war. What can be done to ensure that millions of people who live on one continent do not become collateral victims of a war in another part of the globe? What alternative do we have but to build a more inclusive and equitable international order—currently a distant goal as conflict rages, particularly in the Ukraine, and with sabres rattling over Taiwan?

In the words of Russian war journalist Elena Kostyuchenko, war is like cancer. It spreads easily and no one knows how to stop it.[12] Mediators have the merit of trying to do so despite the obstacles, and will play an essential role in this multipolar and fragmented world, building compromises between a growing array of participants.

NOTES

PREFACE TO THE ENGLISH EDITION

1. Maria Fantappie and Vali Nasr, 'A New Order in the Middle East?', *Foreign Affairs*, New York, March 22, 2023.
2. Samir Saran, 'The new world—shaped by self-interest', *Indian Express*, Noida (India), May 23, 2023.
3. 2.24 trillion dollars, or +3.7 per cent in real terms compared to 2021. 'World military expenditure reaches new record high as European spending surges', Stockholm International Peace Research Institute, April 24, 2023.

1. EXPLORING GREY AREAS

1. Pierre Hazan, *Judging War, Judging History*, Stanford University Press, 2010.
2. 'The ICTY renders its final judgement in the Prlić et al. appeal case', ICTY press release, The Hague, 29 November 2017, https://www.icty.org/en/press/the-icty-renders-its-final-judgement-in-the-prlić-et-al-appeal-case.
3. 'Slobodan Praljak suicide: War criminal "took cyanide" in Hague court', BBC, 1 December 2017, https://www.bbc.com/news/world-europe-42204587.
4. Primo Levi, *The Drowned and the Saved*, translated from

the Italian by Raymond Rosenthal, Simon & Schuster Paperbacks, New York, 1986 (1988).

5. Albert Camus, 'Sauver les corps', *Combat*, 20 November 1946, p. 615.

6. As Uyangoda aptly put it, 'Failed and inconclusive attempts at resolving the conflict have not led to sustainable de-escalation but have instead reconstituted the conflict, redefining its parameters and making the possible paths to peace narrower. Peace negotiations have been occasions for the governments of Sri Lanka and the LTTE to discover new differences, explore new enmities, and reinforce existing antagonisms' (Jayadeva Uyangoda, 'Government–LTTE Peace Negotiations in 2002–2005 and the Clash of State Formation Projects', in Jonathan Goodhand, Jonathan Spencer and Benedikt Korf (eds), *Conflict and Peacebuilding in Sri Lanka: Caught in the Peace Trap?*, Routledge, London, 2011, pp. 16–38). See also Sandra Destradi and Johannes Vüllers, *The Consequences of Failed Mediation in Civil Wars: Assessing the Sri Lankan Case*, GIGA Working Papers No. 202, German Institute of Global and Area Studies, Hamburg, August 2012, https/www.files.ethz.ch/isn/151687/wp202_destradi-vuellers.

2. SHOULD WE NEGOTIATE WITH THE DEVIL?

1. Pawel Florkiewicz, Michel Rose, '"Nobody negotiated with Hitler", Polish PM says, berating France's Macron over Putin talk's', Reuters, 4 April 2022, https://www.reuters.com/world/europe/nobody-negotiated-with-hitler-polish-pm-says-berating-frances-macron-over-putin-2022-04-04/.

NOTES pp. [19–25]

2. Live recording, 'Guerre en Ukraine, en direct: les témoignages de massacre à Boutcha et Borodianka se multiplient, la Russie dénonce une « mise en scène » mais n'apporte pas de preuve', *Le Monde*, 7 April 2022.

3. Devan Cole, 'Zelensky: "I'm ready for negotiations with Putin, but if they fail, it could mean "a third World War"', edition.cnn.com, 20 March 2022, https://edition.cnn.com/2022/03/20/politics/zelensky-putin-ukraine-negotiations-war-cnntv/index.html.

4. 'Seule "la diplomatie" mettra fin à la guerre en Ukraine, assure Volodymyr Zelensky', *Le Temps* and *AFP*, 21 May 2022.

5. Paul Ricoeur, 'Le paradoxe politique', *Esprit*, May 1957, No. 250, pp. 721–745.

6. Winston Churchill "The Second World War" (1950) vol. 3, ch. 20.

7. David Lanz, 'Northern Uganda, Juba Talks', in *Unpacking the Mystery of Mediation in African Peace Processes*, Mediation Support Project, Swisspeace and CSS, 2008, http://www.swisspeace.ch/fileadmin/user_upload/Media/Publications/Journals_Articles/Aberg__Annika__Unpacking_the_Mystery_of_Mediation.pdf.

8. '*Nam pirata non est ex perduellium numero definitus, sed communis hostis omnium; cum hoc nec fides debet nec ius iu- randum esse commune.*' Marcus Tullius Cicero, *De Officiis*, Book III, Ch. XXIX, 107.

9. Hannah Arendt, *Eichmann in Jerusalem: A Report on the Banality of Evil*, Viking Press, 1963.

10. Pentagon Briefing with Secretary Rumsfeld, 19 November 2001, https://www.washingtonpost.com/wp-srv/nation/

specials/attacked/transcripts/rumsfeldtext_111901. html.

11. Jay S. Bybee, Memorandum for John Rizzo, Acting General Counsel of the Central Intelligence Agency, 1 August 2002.

12. Hannah Arendt, *Totalitarianism*, Part 3 of *The Origins of Totalitarianism*, Harcourt, 1976.

3. FROM MORALITY TO HUBRIS

1. Herodotus "The Histories" Book 7, Ch. 10.

2. Security Council resolution 808 of 22 February 1993, establishing the International Criminal Tribunal for the former Yugoslavia.

3. Francis Fukuyama, *The End of History and the Last Man*, Free Press, 1992.

4. Boutros Boutros-Ghali, *An Agenda for Peace. Preventive Diplomacy, Peacemaking and Peace-keeping*, United Nations, 1992, p. 8.

5. David Harland, *The Lost Art of Peacemaking*, Centre for Humanitarian Dialogue, 2018, https://www.hdcentre.org/ publications/the-lost-art-of-peacemaking/.

6. Available at www.icc-cpi.int/sites/default/files/RS-Eng. pdf.

7. I discuss this in detail in an earlier book, *La paix contre la justice? Comment reconstruire un Etat avec des criminels de guerre*, GRIP/André Versaille, 2010.

8. Richard Goldstone, 'Bringing War Criminals to Justice in an Ongoing War', in Jonathan Moore, *Hard Choices, Moral Dilemmas in Humanitarian Intervention*, Rowman & Littlefield Publishers, 1998, p. 204.

9. Ibid, p. 198.
10. Pierre Hazan, *La paix contre la justice?*, op. cit., note 6.
11. While Crane was going around saving international justice, the United States was applying a perfectly cynical and brutal policy in the same field. It was the strongest and biggest political and financial supporter of the ad hoc tribunals, but also the most implacable adversary of the International Criminal Court. Indeed, the American Service-Members Protection Act authorises the President to use 'all means necessary and appropriate to bring about the release of any U.S. or allied personnel being detained or imprisoned by, on behalf of, or at the request of the International Criminal Court'.
12. Security Council resolution 808, op. cit., note 1.
13. All of them fiercely opposed to the Russian invasion, namely all the Member States of the European Union, Switzerland, Australia, Canada, New Zealand, Colombia and Costa Rica.
14. Khan was pleased to announce 'the largest ever single field deployment' by the Court to collect evidence of war crimes and draw up indictments. He expressed sincere appreciation to certain Western countries, in particular the Netherlands, for funding most of the forty-two investigators sent to Ukraine, giving the impression that the Court was happy to be bought off. Apart from the fact that the Netherlands hosts the Court's seat and is a NATO member, it is engaged in ongoing litigation with Russia, which has never acknowledged—despite a trial by a Dutch court—that it was responsible for firing the surface-to-air missile that shot down a Malaysian Airlines

plane over the separatist zone of Ukraine on 17 July 2014 and killed 298 passengers, two-thirds of whom were Dutch. ('ICC Prosecutor Karim A.A. Khan QC announces deployment of forensics and investigative team to Ukraine, welcomes strong cooperation with the Government of the Netherlands', press release, 17 May 2022, https://www.icc-cpi.int/news/icc-prosecutor-karim-aa-khan-qc-announces-deployment-forensics-and-investigative-team-ukraine).

15. Philippe Ricard, 'Les alliés de l'Ukraine divergent sur la qualification des crimes commis en Ukraine', *Le Monde*, 14 April 2022. French President Macron, who hoped that France would be able to act as a mediator, ventured to say that 'an escalation of words would not help bring peace'.

16. Daniel Boffey, Shaun Walker, Philip Olterman, 'Biden: For God's sake, "Butcher" Putin cannot be allowed to stay in power', *The Guardian*, 27 March 2022, www.theguardian.com/us-news/2022/mar/26/biden-butcher-putin-cannot-be-allowed-to-stay-in-power.

17. Andrew Fink, 'What's Behind Dmitry Medvedev's Nuclear Saber-Rattling?', *The Dispatch*, 12 July 2022, https://thedispatch.com/p/whats-behind-dmitry-medvedevs-nuclear.

4. TO NEGOTIATE OR NOT TO NEGOTIATE?

1. The full text of President Bush's address to a joint session of Congress and the nation, 20 September 2001, is available at www.washingtonpost.com/wp-srv/nation/specials/attacked/transcripts/bushaddress_092001.html.

2. George W. Bush, second inaugural address, 20 January

2005, www.govinfo.gov/content/pkg/CREC-2005-01-20/pdf/CREC-2005-01-20-pt1-PgS101-5.pdf.

3. Security Council resolution 1373, 28 September 2001.

4. Nathalie Janne d'Othée, 'Liste des organisations terroristes, quand l'UE s'emmêle', *Orient XXI*, 10 January 2022, p. 5286, https://orientxxi.info/magazine/liste-des-organisations-terroristes-quand-l-union-europeenne-s-emmele.

5. Antony J. Blinken, 'Revocation of the Terrorist Designations of the Revolutionary Armed Forces of Colombia (FARC) and Additional Terrorist Designations', State Department press statement, 30 November 2021, www.state.gov/revocation-of-the-terrorist-designations-of-the-revolutionary-armed-forces-of-colombia-farc-and-additional-terrorist-designation.

6. See Magnus Lundgren, Isak Svenson, 'The surprising decline of international mediation in armed conflicts', *Research and Politics*, April–June 2020.

7. Which explains why only 17% benefit from mediation.

8. See Ben Parker, 'A Q&A with the pro-Israel US lawyer rattling NGOs on counter-terror compliance', *The New Humanitarian*, 25 September 2018, www.thenewhumanitarian.org/interview/2018/09/25/qa-pro-israel-us-lawyer-rattling-ngos-counter-terror-compliance, and 'Manhattan U.S. Attorney Announces Settlement with Norwegian Not-For-Profit, Resolving Claims that It Provided Material Support to Iran, Hamas, and Other Prohibited Parties under US Laws', US Department of Justice, 3 April 2018, www.justice.gov/usao-sdny/pr/manhattan-us-attorney-announces-settlement-norwegian-not-profit-resolving-claims-it.

9. Rory McCarthy and Ian Williams, 'UN was pummelled into submission, says outgoing Middle East special envoy', *The Guardian*, 13 June 2007, www.theguardian.com/world/2007/jun/13/usa.israel1.

10. The Nobel Peace Prize for 2008 to Martti Ahtisaari, press release, 10 October 2008, www.nobelprize.org/prizes/peace/2008/press-release/.

11. Julia Palmiano Federer, 'Cowboys or Mavericks? The normative agency of NGO mediators', in C. Turner and M. Wählisch (eds), *Rethinking Peace Mediation: Challenges of Contemporary Peacemaking Practice*, Bristol University Press, 2021.

12. Véronique Dudouet, 'Mediating Peace with Proscribed Armed Groups', United States Institute of Peace, *Special Report*, No. 237, 2010.

13. Jonathan Powell, *Talking to Terrorists: How to End Armed Conflicts*, Bodley Head, 2014.

5. THE END OF PAX AMERICANA

1. Coined by the neo-conservative Robert Kagan, *Of Paradise and Power: America and Europe in the New World Order*, Vintage Books, 2003.

2. Gilad Ben-Nun, 'A Synchronic Dialogue and the Emerging Concept of Legal Security in Africa', in Francis Onditi, Gilad Ben-Nun, Edmond M. Were and Israel Nyaburi Nyadera, *Reimagining Security Communities*, Palgrave Macmillan Cham, 2021, p. 352.

3. Anne Orford, in Gilad Ben-Nun, ibid.

4. Vladimir Putin, 'Prepared Remarks at the 43rd Munich Conference on Security Policy', 10 February 2007, http://en.kremlin.ru/events/president/transcripts/24034.

5. Barack Obama, *A Promised Land*, Penguin Books, 2020, pp. 328–329.

6. Peter Baker, 'The US-Russian ties still fall short of "Reset" Goal', *New York Times*, 9 September 2013.

7. Quoted by Gilad Ben Nun, 2021, op. cit., note 2.

8. The law of armed conflict is made up of treaties (the Geneva Conventions and their Additional Protocols are the main ones) and customary international law.

9. According to the map of peace agreements drawn up by the University of Notre Dame, which does not include global peace agreements.

10. See David Lanz, *The Responsibility to Protect in Darfur, From Forgotten Conflict to Global Cause and Back*, Routledge, 2019.

11. Laurie Nathan, *No Ownership, No Peace: The Darfur Peace Agreement*, Working Paper No. 5, Crisis States Research Centre, London School of Economics, 2006.

12. Christine Cheng, Jonathan Goodhand, Patrick Meehan, 'Elite Bargains and Political Deals Project', Stabilisation Unit, UK Foreign Office, 2018.

13. Roger McGinty, 'Indigenous Peace-Making Versus the Liberal Peace', *Cooperation and Conflict*, Vol. 43, No. 2 (June 2008); Roland Paris, 'Peacebuilding and the Limits of Liberal Internationalism', *International Security*, Vol. 22, No. 2 (Fall, 1997), pp. 54–89, https://www.jstor.org/stable/2539367.

14. United Nations, 'Report of the Secretary-General on enhancing mediation and its support activities' (S/2009/189), 8 April 2009, para. 61, https://peacemaker.un.org/sites/peacemaker.un.org/files/SGReport_EnhancingMediation_S2009189%28english%29_0.pdf.

6. FROM COMPROMISE TO COMPLICITY?

1. Paul Ricoeur, speaking with Jean-Marie Muller and François Vaillant, *Alternatives Non Violentes*, No. 80, October 1991.

2. Rony Brauman, 'Catastrophes naturelles: "Do something!"', in Claire Magone, Michael Neuman, Fabrice Weissman (eds), *Agir à tout prix, Négociations humanitaires: l'expérience de Médecins Sans Frontières*, Éditions La Découverte, 2011.

3. Sylvie Bodineau, in *Anthropen.org*, Paris, Éditions des archives contemporaines, 2017.

4. Jonas Baumann and Govinda Clayton, 'Mediation in violent conflict', *CSS Analyses in Security Policies*, No. 211, June 2017, https://css.ethz.ch/content/dam/ethz/special-interest/gess/cis/center-for-securities-studies/pdfs/CSSAnalyse211-EN.pdf.

5. Frédéric Bobin, Louis Imbert, 'Le "deal" de Donald Trump entre le Maroc et Israël', *Le Monde*, 11 December 2020, www.lemonde.fr/afrique/article/2020/12/11/le-deal-de-donald-trump-entre-le-maroc-et-israel_6063018_3212.html.

6. Diderot et d'Alembert, *L'Encyclopédie*, définition du médiateur, vol. X, 1765, p. 294a, http://enccre.academie-sciences.fr/encyclopedie/article/v10–743–1/.

7. Marion Harroff-Tavel, 'Neutrality and Impartiality. The importance of these principles for the International Red Cross and Red Crescent Movement and the difficulties involved in applying them', *International Review of the Red Cross*, Vol. 29, Issue 273, December 1989, p. 543.

8. Berghof Foundation, Vision, mission and principles, https://berghof-foundation.org/about/vision.

9. Proposals set out on paper with no official letterhead and

therefore signed by no one, enabling the parties to talk about them more freely than if they came from the enemy.

10. Johan Birger Essen Dahlerus testimony, Nuremberg trials, TMWC IX, pp. 470–471. In the weeks before the war, while the Third Reich was actively preparing to attack, Göring gave Dahlerus a mission: to inform London that the Third Reich pledged not to attack Poland in exchange for the restoration of Danzig to Germany and the organisation of a referendum in the 'Polish corridor' leading to the city.

11. Ibid.

12. Ghassan Salamé, 'On the failure of the international community to stop wars' [podcast], The Mediator's Studio, Episode 2, Season 1, Centre for Humanitarian Dialogue, 30 June 2020, www.hdcentre.org/podcasts/ghassan-salam-on-the-failures-of-the-international-community-to-stop-wars/.

13. Paul Ricoeur, *Soi-même comme un autre*, Seuil, 1990.

14. Kant defines categorial imperatives as commands or moral laws all persons must follow, regardless of their desires or extenuating circumstances. As morals, these imperatives are binding on everyone.

15. See Todd and Hans-Joachim Lauth, 'Trade-offs in the Political Real: How Important Are Trade-Offs in Politics?', *Politics and Governance*, Vol. 7, No. 4 (2019). In the humanitarian field, see Magone, Neuman and Weissman, op. cit., note 2.

16. Interview Philippe Gaillard, *Frontline*, PBS, 1 April 2004, https://www.pbs.org/wgbh/pages/frontline/shows/ghosts/interviews/gaillard.html.

7. NEUTRALITY IN THE FACE OF GENOCIDE

1. Max Huber, 'Red Cross and Neutrality', offprint of *Revue internationale de la Croix-Rouge*, No. 206, May 1936, https://library.icrc.org/library/docs/DOC/DOC_00197.pdf.
2. Ibid., pp. 5 and 7.
3. Irène Herrmann and Daniel Palmieri, 'Le Comité international de la Croix-Rouge et les camps de concentration nazis, 1933–1939', *La contemporaine*, 2009/3, No. 95, pp. 65–74.
4. See Gerald Steinacher, *Humanitarians at War: the Red Cross in the Shadow of the Holocaust*, Oxford University Press, 2017.
5. The International Committee of the Red Cross was directed by an executive Committee, hereafter the Committee (called today the Assembly).
6. Fabrice Cahen, 'Le Comité International de la Croix-Rouge (CICR) et les visites de camps', *Revue d'Histoire de la Shoah*, 2001/2, No. 172, pp. 7–62.
7. Lemkin's interest was spurred after he learned about the Armenian massacres (1915–1917) and discovered that no international laws existed to prosecute the Ottoman leaders who had ordered their perpetration. In his 1933 Madrid proposal, he proposed the creation of a multilateral convention making the extermination of human groups an international crime on a par with slavery, piracy and other universally recognised 'offences against the law of nations'. At the time, he called the crime 'Acts of Barbarity'. Ten years later, in 1943, he would coin a new word—'genocide'—

also as part of his analysis of German occupation policies in Europe and the persecution of Jews and Gypsies.

8. Isabelle Vonèche Cardia, 'Les raisons du silence du Comité international de la Croix-Rouge face aux deportations', *Revue d'histoire de la Shoah*, 2015/2, No. 203, pp. 87–122.

9. Efforts to improve the treatment of prisoners of war were first made in the nineteenth century. Then, in 1929, building on the agreements reached between countries during the First World War, the states adopted the Geneva Convention relative to the Treatment of Prisoners of War, the first multilateral treaty aimed specifically at protecting prisoners of war and the precursor to the 1949 Third Geneva Convention relative to the Treatment of Prisoners of War. The 1949 Convention would not have extended automatic protection to Soviet and German POWs. The Germans believed that Soviet POWs did not deserve protection because the USSR had not ratified the 1929 Convention. The Soviets reciprocated vis-à-vis their German POWs.

10. Huber did not voice an opinion in the initial consultation.

11. Max Huber, op. cit., note 1, pp. 6–7.

12. Isabelle Vonèche Cardia, op. cit., note 7.

13. International Committee of the Red Cross, plenary meeting of 14 October 1942 at 3 p.m. at the former Hôtel Métropole, minutes 6/1942.

14. Ibid.

15. The morality of an action is to be judged solely by its consequences.

16. Ibid.

17. Ibid.
18. François Bugnon, 'Entre histoire et mémoire, le CICR et les camps de concentration et d'extermination nazis', November 2002, statement delivered in French to mark the opening of the exhibition *Mémoire des camps* (Remembering the camps) at the International Museum of the Red Cross and Red Crescent, www.icrc.org/fr/doc/resources/documents/misc/68xejs.htm. In reaction to the precedent set during World War II, the ICRC drew up a new policy on the denunciation of war crimes.

8. BOSNIA: FAREWELL TO NEUTRALITY

1. Over twenty resolutions, see https://en.wikipedia.org/wiki/List_of_United_Nations_Security_Council_Resolutions_related_to_the_conflicts_in_former_Yugoslavia.
2. United Nations, Report of the Secretary-General pursuant to General Assembly resolution 53/35. The fall of Srebrenica (A/54/549), 15 November 1999, https://digitallibrary.un.org/record/372298?ln=en.
3. George F. Will, 'A Dog In That Fight'?, *Newsweek*, 6 November 1995, www.newsweek.com/dog-fight-183518.
4. A Blue helmet / UN peace-keeper is a soldier who is deployed by the UN to prevent conflict or maintain or restore peace. The United Nations Protection Force (UNPROFOR) in former Yugoslavia was formed in February 1992. UNPROFOR was created by UN Security Council resolution 743 on 21 February 1992 during the Croatian War of Independence. The initial mandate of UNPROFOR was to ensure stable conditions for peace

talks. The mandate was enlarged a number of times and extended to Bosnia-Herzegovina to protect Sarajevo airport, humanitarian convoys, safe areas... UNPROFOR ended its mandate in March 1995. UNPROFOR was composed of nearly 39,000 personnel. It consisted of troops from Argentina, Australia, Bangladesh, Belgium, Brazil, Canada, Colombia, Czech Republic, Denmark, Egypt, Estonia, Finland, France, Germany, Ghana, India, Indonesia, Ireland, Italy, Jordan, Kenya, Lithuania, Luxembourg, Malaysia, Nepal, Netherlands, New Zealand, Nigeria, Norway, Pakistan, Poland, Portugal, the Russian Federation, Slovak Republic, Spain, Sweden, Switzerland, Tunisia, Turkey, Ukraine, the United Kingdom and the United States.

5. Pierre Hazan, *Justice in a Time of War: The True Story Behind the International Criminal Tribunal for the Former Yugoslavia*, Texas A&M, 2004.

6. In the words of David Owen, European Community mediator at the conference on the former Yugoslavia (see Katja Favretto, 'Should Peacemakers take Sides? Major Power Mediation, Coercion, and Bias', *The American Political Science Review*, Vol. 103, No. 2 (May 2009), pp. 248–263, at p. 248).

7. Security Council resolution 824 of 6 May 1993 lists the six UN 'safe areas'.

8. Council adopts EU strategy on Syria, press release, Council of the European Union, 3 April 2017, www.consilium. europa.eu/fr/press/press-releases/2017/04/03/fac-conclusions-syria/.

9. Larry Hollingworth and Tony Land, interview, 25 January 2022.

10. Jacques de Maio, interview, 25 January 2022.

11. HD receives Carnegie Wateler Peace Prize at ceremony marking track record of conflict mediation, acceptance speech by David Harland, The Hague, 3 November 2022, https://hdcentre.org/news/hd-receives-carnegie-wateler-peace-prize-for-track-record-of-conflict-mediation/.

12. United Nations, Report of the Secretary-General, op. cit., note 2, para. 482.

13. The formal name of the Dayton Accords is the General Framework Agreement for Peace in Bosnia and Herzegovina, https://www.osce.org/files/f/documents/e/0/126173.pdf.

14. United Nations, Report of the Independent Inquiry into the actions of the United Nations during the 1994 genocide in Rwanda, S/1999/1257, 16 December 1999, https://www.securitycouncilreport.org/atf/cf/%7B65BFCF9B-6D27-4E9C-8CD3-CF6E4FF96FF9%7D/POC%20S19991257.pdf.

15. Ibid., para. 499.

16. Ibid., para. 505.

17. Ibid., para. 502.

18. United Nations press release SG/SM/6552 AFR 56, 6 May 1998.

9. SYRIA: MISSION IMPOSSIBLE

1. The mandate was established by the Geneva Communiqué of 30 June 2012, and confirmed in Security Council resolution 2254 of 18 December 2015.

2. In 2011, President Obama invited Assad 'to get out of the way' (see https://obamawhitehouse.archives.gov/blog/

2011/08/18/president-obama-future-syria-must-be-deter-
mined-its-people-president-bashar-al-assad). The European
Union also demanded that President Assad be removed
from power. According to the French Minister for Foreign
Affairs, Laurent Fabius, 'No one can imagine for even an
instant that Assad will be part of the government or that
he can establish a neutral environment' ('Accord à Genève
sur les principes d'une transition en Syrie', *Le Monde avec
AFP et Reuters*, 30 June 2012.

3. The Arab League started the mediation before being joined
   by the United Nations, which took over its steerage.

4. Kofi Annan Foundation, Press conference by Joint Special
   Envoy for Syria, 2 August 2012, www.kofiannanfounda-
   tion.org/foundation-news/press-conference-by-joint-spe-
   cial-envoy-for-syria/.

5. Independent International Commission of Inquiry on the
   Syrian Arab Republic, *Sieges as a Weapon of War. Encircle,
   Starve, Surrender, Evacuate*, 29 May 2018, para. 9, www.
   ohchr.org/sites/default/files/Documents/HRBodies/
   HRCouncil/CoISyria/PolicyPaperSieges_29May2018.
   pdf.

6. The report is mentioned by several authors. See David
   Kenner, 'Rewriting Syria's War', *Foreign Policy*, 18 December
   2014; James Traub, 'Bashar Al-Assad and the Devil's
   Bargain', *Foreign Policy*, 14 November 2014; David
   Ignatius, 'A Plan to Save Syria', *Washington Post*, 4 November
   2014.

7. Specifically, 'to build first some political process at a local
   level and then eventually at the national level, give some
   hope to the local population', see Transcript—Press

Stakeout: UN Special Envoy for Syria, Mr Staffan de Mistura, New York, 30 October 2014, https://reliefweb.int/report/syrian-arab-republic/transcript-press-stake-out-un-special-envoy-syria-mr-staffan-de-mistura.

8. Ibid.

9. As confirmed in Security Council resolution 2254.

10. See Sara Hellmüller, 'Peacemaking in a shifting world order: A macro-level analysis of UN mediation in Syria', *Review of International Studies*, 2022, 48:3, pp. 543–559.

11. Mouin Rabbani, 'Not much special in UN Middle East Missions', Institute for Palestine Studies, 2015.

12. United Nations General Assembly, Report of the Independent International Commission of Inquiry on the Syrian Arab Republic, Human Rights Council document A/HRC/36/55, 8 August 2017, para. 18, https://documents-dds-ny.un.org/doc/UNDOC/GEN/G17/234/18/PDF/G1723418.pdf?OpenElement.

13. Independent International Commission of Inquiry on the Syrian Arab Republic, op. cit., note 5, para. 9.

14. United Nations General Assembly, op. cit., note 12, para. 18.

15. Council adopts EU strategy on Syria, press release, Council of the European Union, 3 April 2017, www.consilium.europa.eu/fr/press/press-releases/2017/04/03/fac-conclusions-syria/.

16. Ibid.

17. United Nations General Assembly, 'Human right abuses and international humanitarian law violations in the Syrian Arab Republic', 21 July 2016–28 February 2017, Conference room paper of the International Commission

of Investigation, Human Rights Council document A_HRC_34_CRP.3_E, 27 February 2017.

18. United Nations General Assembly, 'Report of the Independent International Commission of Inquiry on the Syrian Arab Republic', Human Rights Council document A/HCR/34/64, 2 February 2017, para. 93, https://documents-dds-ny.un.org/doc/UNDOC/GEN/G17/026/63/PDF/G1702663.pdf?OpenElement.

19. Areeb Ullah, 'La Croix-Rouge défend son rôle dans les évacuations d'Alep suite au rapport accablant de l'ONU', *Middle East Eye*, 2 March 2017, www.middleeasteye.net/fr/reportages/la-croix-rouge-defend-son-role-dans-les-evacuations-dalep-suite-un-rapport-accablant-de.

20. Ibid.

10. THE SAHEL: TALKING WITH JIHADISTS

1. The fourth after those of 1962–1964, 1990–1995 and 2007–2009.

2. A former member of Gaddafi's Islamic Legion, Ghali, a Tuareg, had fought in Chad and Lebanon before becoming active in Tuareg rebellions against the Malian government in the 1980s. In 1988, he founded the Popular Movement for the Liberation of Azawad and led the 1990–1996 rebellion. He subsequently intervened to obtain the release of Western hostages being held by the Salafist Group for Preaching and Combat (GSPC, the forerunner to Al-Qaeda in the Islamic Maghreb) in 1999 and 2003.

3. Interview of Macron in *Jeune Afrique*, 20 November 2020.

4. Agreement for Peace and Reconciliation in Mali Resulting from the Algiers Process, 2015, available in English at www.

un.org/en/pdfs/EN-ML_150620_Accord-pour-la-paix-et-la-reconciliation-au-Mali_Issu-du-Processus-d%27Alger.pdf.

5. 'Mali's Algiers Peace Agreement, Five Years On: An Uneasy Calm', International Crisis Group, 24 June 2020, https://www.crisisgroup.org/africa/sahel/mali/laccord-dalger-cinq-ans-apres-un-calme-precaire-dont-il-ne-faut-pas-se-satisfaire.

6. Ferdaous Bouhlel, *(Ne pas) dialoguer avec les groupes djihadistes au Mali*, Berghof Foundation, 2020.

7. 'La France doit rompre avec la rhétorique martiale qui prévaut au Sahel', *Le Monde*, 21 February 2018.

8. Ibid.

9. Ferdaous Bouhlel, op. cit., note 8.

10. Ibid.

11. 'Burkina Faso: a million students deprived of school because of the jihadists', Africanews with AFP, 24 November 2022, https://www.africanews.com/2022/11/24/burkina-faso-a-million-students-deprived-of-school-because-of-the-jihadists//.

12. In international law and international relations, the term 'good offices' under the UN Charter refers to all diplomatic and humanitarian initiatives by a third country or a neutral institution whose purpose is to resolve a bilateral or international conflict or to bring the parties to the negotiating table.

13. Centre for Humanitarian Dialogue, *La médiation des conflits locaux au Sahel, Burkina Faso, Mali et Niger*, Geneva, 2022. Centre for Humanitarian Dialogue, peace agreement signed between the Fulani and Dogon communi-

ties, https://www.hdcentre.org/fr/updates/fulani-and-dogon-communities-from-koro-sign-a-peace-agreement-in-the-mopti-region-of-mali/; peace agreement signed between the Idurfane and Ibolgoltan communities on the border between Mali and Niger, 2018, https://www.hdcentre.org/fr/updates/signature-dun-accord-de-paix-entre-les-communautes-idourfane-et-ibogolitane-a-la-frontiere-entre-le-mali-et-le-niger/; peace agreement signed between the Fulani and Mahamid Arab communities in the Diffa region, 2019, https://www.hdcentre.org/fr/updates/signing-of-a-peace-agreement-between-fulani-and-mahamid-arab-communities-in-the-diffa-region-of-niger/.

14. Centre for Humanitarian Dialogue, op. cit., note 12.

15. 'Le président malien confirme l'ouverture d'un dialogue avec les chefs djihadistes', France 24, 10 February 2020, https://www.france24.com/fr/afrique/20200210-exclusif-le-président-malien-ibk-confirme-l-ouverture-d-un-dialogue-avec-des-chefs-jihadistes.

16. 'Sahel 2021: Communal Wars, Broken Ceasefires, and Shifting Frontlines', ACLED, 17 June 2021, https://acleddata.com/2021/06/17/sahel-2021-communal-wars-broken-ceasefires-and-shifting-frontlines/.

17. Sam Mednick, 'Les pourparlers de paix secrets au Burkina Faso et le cessez-le-feu fragile des djihadistes', *The New Humanitarian*, 11 March 2021, https://www.thenewhumanitarian.org/fr/2021/03/11/exclusif-les-pourparlers-de-paix-secrets-au-burkina-faso-et-le-cessez-le-feu-fragile-des.

18. 'Niger: la stratégie du dialogue avec les jihadistes pour

retrouver la paix', FranceInfo avec AFP, 18 March 2022, https://www.francetvinfo.fr/monde/afrique/niger/niger-la-strategie-du-dialogue-avec-les-jihadistes-pour-retrouver-la-paix_5024541.html.

19. International Crisis Group, *Mali: Enabling Dialogue with the Jihadist Coalition JNIM*, Africa Report No. 306, Brussels, 10 December 2021.

20. International Crisis Group, *Speaking with the 'Bad Guys': Toward Dialogue with Central Mali's Jihadists*, Africa Report No. 276, Brussels, 28 May 2019, https://www.crisisgroup.org/fr/africa/sahel/mali/276-speaking-bad-guys-toward-dialogue-central-malis-jihadists.

21. 'Dialogue possible with certain Sahel Jihadists: UN chief', *The Defense Post*, 19 October 2020.

22. Cited by the International Crisis Group, op. cit., note 16.

CONCLUSION: THE DEREGULATION OF FORCE

1. Rémy Ourdan, 'Guerre en Ukraine: la visite d'Antonio Guterres marquée par le bombardement de Kiev', *Le Monde*, 29 April 2022.

2. David Gritten, 'Israel and Lebanon agree "historic" maritime border deal, US says', BBC News, 11 October 2022, https://www.bbc.com/news/world-middle-east-63222903.

3. 'United Nations, Beacon on the Black Sea, Black Sea Grain Initiative Joint Coordination Centre', press release, 27 July 2022, www.un.org/en/black-sea-grain-initiative.

4. Fatma Tanis, 'Russia and Ukraine renew a grain export deal to help the hungry and keep prices down', NPR, 17 November 2022, https://www.nprillinois.org/2022-11-17/

russia-and-ukraine-renew-a-grain-export-deal-to-help-the-hungry-and-keep-prices-down.

5. Antonio Gramsci (1891–1937) was an Italian Marxist philosopher, journalist, linguist, writer and politician. He was a founding member and one-time leader of the Italian Communist Party.

6. Amanda Seitz and Arjieta Lajka, 'Russian media campaign falsely claims Bucha deaths are fakes', AP, 6 April 2022, https://apnews.com/article/russia-ukraine-kyiv-business-media-facebook-21d36ea4370bab98b1cc93baa0815dd8.

7. 'HD Citizens' Charter in Bosnia and Herzegovina sets standards for social meida conduct in run-up to elections', HD, 1 August 2022, https://hdcentre.org/news/hd-citizens-charter-in-bosnia-and-herzegovina-sets-standards-for-social-media-conduct-in-run-up-to-elections/.

8. 'Time for a new Push for Peace and Reconciliation', UN press release, 23 May 2020, https://www.un.org/en/globalceasefire.

9. United Nations, 'Covid-19: les effets de l'appel de l'ONU au "cessez-le-feu mondial"', press release, 6 April 2020, https://www.un.org/fr/coronavirus-covid-19-fr/covid-19-les-effets-de-lappel-de-lonu-au-«-cessez-le-feu-mondial-».

10. 'Social media in peace mediation, a practical framework', UN Mediation Support Unit and Swisspeace, June 2021; 'Social media code of conduct: reflections for mediators', 18 August 2020, Centre for Humanitarian Dialogue, www.hdcentre.org/updates/social-media-codes-of-conduct-reflections-for-mediators/.

11. Sabrim Kassam, 'Mediation Perspectives: Dealing with Organized Crimes', CSS blog, 30 January 2015, https:// isnblog.ethz.ch/css-blog/mediation-perspectives-dealing-with-organized-crime.
12. Quoted by Nataliya Sekretareva, '"From Russia with hate": l'immense besoin de justice dans la guerre en Ukraine, *Le Temps*, 12 July 2022, www.letemps.ch/opin-ions/from-russia-with-hate-limmense-besoin-justice-guerre-ukraine.

FURTHER READING

Arendt, Hannah, *Totalitarianism*, Part 3 of *The Origins of Totalitarianism*, Harcourt, 1976.

Arendt, Hannah, *Eichmann in Jerusalem: A Report on the Banality of Evil*, Viking Press, 1963.

Autesserre, Severine, *The Frontlines of Peace*, Oxford University Press, 2021.

Bauer, Yehuad, *Jews for Sale: Jewish Negotiations 1933–1945*, Yale University Press, 1994.

Bouhlel Ferdaous, *(Ne pas) dialogue avec les groupes djihadistes au Mali*, Berghof Foundation, 2020.

Boutros-Ghali, Boutros, *An Agenda for Peace. Preventive Diplomacy, Peacemaking and Peace-keeping*, United Nations, 1992.

Brauman, Rony, *Le dilemme*, Textuel, 1996.

Camus, Albert, 'Neither Victims nor Executioners', in *Between Hell and Reason: Essays from the Resistance Newspaper* Combat, *1944–1947*, selected and translated by Alexandre de Gramont, Wesleyan University Press, 1991.

Cheng, Christine, Goodhand, Jonathan and Meehan, Patrick, 'Elite Bargains and Political Deals Project', Stabilisation Unit, UK Foreign Office, 2018.

FURTHER READING

Dudouet, Véronique, 'Mediating Peace with Proscribed Armed Groups', United States Institute of Peace, *Special Report*, No. 237, 2010.

Harland, David, 'The Lost Art of Peacemaking', Centre for Humanitarian Dialogue, 2018.

Harroff-Tavel, Marion, 'Neutrality and Impartiality. The importance of these principles for the International Red Cross and Red Crescent Movement and the difficulties involved in applying them', *International Review of the Red Cross*, Vol. 29, Issue 273, December 1989.

Hazan, Pierre, *Judging War, Judging History—Behind Truth and Reconciliation*, translated by Sarah Meyer de Stadelhofen, Stanford University Press, 2010.

———, *La paix contre la justice?, Comment reconstruire un Etat avec des criminels de guerre*, GRIP/André Versaille, 2010.

———, *Justice in a Time of War: The True Story Behind the International Criminal Tribunal for the former Yugoslavia*, translated by J.T. Snyder, Texas A&M University Press, 2004.

Hellmüller, Sara, 'Peacemaking in a shifting world order: A macro-level analysis of UN mediation in Syria', *Review of International Studies*, 2022, 48:3, pp. 543–559.

Herrman, Irène and Palmieri, Daniel, 'Le Comité international de la Croix-Rouge et les camps de concentration nazis, 1933–1939', *La contemporaine*, 2009/3 No. 95, pp. 65–74.

Holbrooke, Richard, *To End a War*, The Modern Library, 1998.

Howard, Michael, *The Invention of Peace*, Profile Books, 2001.

182

Huber, Max, 'Red Cross and Neutrality', offprint of *Revue internationale de la Croix-Rouge*, No. 206, May 1936.

Lanz, David, *The Responsibility to Protect in Darfur, From Forgotten Conflict to Global Cause and Back*, Routledge, 2019.

———, 'Northern Uganda, Juba Talks', in *Unpacking the Mystery of Mediation in African Peace Processes*, Mediation Support Project, Swisspeace and CSS, 2008.

Levi, Primo, *Les naufragés et les rescapés*, Gallimard, 1989.

Magone, Claire, Neuman, Michael and Weissman, Fabrice (eds), *Agir à tout prix, Négociations humanitaires: l'expérience de Médecins Sans Frontières*, 2011.

Margalit, Avishai, *On Compromise and Rotten Compromises*, Princeton University Press, 2010.

McGinty, Roger, 'Indigenous Peace-making versus the Liberal Peace', *Cooperation and Conflict*, Vol. 43, No. 2 (June 2008), pp. 139–163.

Moore, Jonathan, *Hard Choices, Moral Dilemmas in Humanitarian Intervention*, Rowman & Littlefield Publishers, 1999.

Nathan, Laurie, 'No ownership, no peace: The Darfur peace agreement', *Crisis States Research Centre*, Working Paper No. 5, London School of Economics, 2006.

Ondit, Francis, Ben-Nun, Gilad, Were, Edmond M. and Nyaburi Nyadera, Israel, *Reimagining Security Communities*, Palgrave Macmillan, 2021.

Palmiano Federer, Julia, 'Cowboys or Mavericks? The normative agency of NGO mediators', in Turner, C. and Wählisch, M. (eds), *Rethinking Peace Mediation: Challenges of Contemporary Peacemaking Practice*, 2021.

Paris, Roland, 'Peacebuilding and the Limits of Liberal Internationalism', *International Security*, Vol. 22, No. 2 (Fall 1997), pp. 54–89.

Powell, Jonathan, *Talking to Terrorists: How to End Armed Conflicts*, Bodley Head, 2014.

Rabbani, Mouin, 'Not much special in UN Middle East Missions', *Institute for Palestine Studies*, 2015.

Ricoeur, Paul, 'Le paradoxe politique', *Esprit*, May 1957, No. 250, pp. 721–745.

———, *Soi-même comme un autre*, Payot, 1990.

———, interview by Jean-Marie Muller and François Vaillant, *Alternatives Non Violentes*, No. 80, October 1991.

Slim, Hugo, *Humanitarian Ethics*, Hurst, 2015.

Steinacher, Gerald, *Humanitarians at War: the Red Cross in the Shadow of the Holocaust*, Oxford University Press, 2017.

Vonèche Cardia, Isabelle, 'Les raisons du silence du Comité international de la Croix-Rouge face aux deportations', *Revue d'histoire de la Shoah*, No. 203, pp. 87–122.

Wieland, Carsten, *Syria and the Neutrality Trap*, I.B. Tauris, 2021.

INDEX

Note: Page numbers followed by "*n*" refer to notes.

11 September 2001 attacks, 14, 24, 41, 53, 146–7

200 Dutch Blue Helmets, 105

Abraham Accords (2020), 149–50

'Acts of Barbarity', 168*n*7

Afghanistan, 58, 142, 147

African Union Commissioner for Peace and Security, 142

African Union, 8, 49, 99, 130

ag Ghali, Iyad, 129, 134–5

Agenda for Peace, An, 31, 139

Agreement for Peace and Reconciliation, 130

Ahtisaari, Martti, 48

al- Nusra Front, 121

al-Assad's regime, 57

Aleppo, 116–17, 121, 122

Alexander VI, Pope, 69

Al-Qaeda in the Islamic Maghreb, 129

al-Qaeda, 129, 134, 136–9

Amelioration of the Condition of the Wounded in Armies in the Field, 82

American hegemony, 30, 53, 59, 118, 145

American hubris, 55–6

American policy, 143–4

American Service-Members Protection Act, 160–1*n*11

Annan, Kofi, 106, 107–9, 113, 116

Ansar Dine (Defenders of
   the Faith), 131–2
   Tuareg rebellion, 128–30
anti-Semitic laws, 82
anti-terrorism, 27–8
Arab League, 57, 112–13
Arab Mahamid community,
   138–9
Arendt, Hannah, 24, 28
Argentina, 170–1n4
Armenian massacres, 168n7
Arusha, 99
al-Assad, Bashar, 112,
   172–3n2
   Assad regime, 112–15
Australia, 170–1n4
Axis powers, 87
'Azawad', 129, 175n2

Bahrain, 149–50
Baker, James, 96
Bamako, 128, 129, 130, 142
Bambara, 140
Ban Ki-moon, 47, 61
Bangladesh, 170–1n4
Bataclan, 134
Bazoum, Mohamed, 141
Belgium, 44, 170–1n4
Ben-Nun, Gilad, 55
Berghof Foundation, 48,
   49–50, 72

Berislav Pušić, 5, 6–7
Berlin Wall, fall of, 30
Berlin, 86, 91
Bernadotte, Count, 93
Bernadotte, Folke, 21
Biden, Joe, 39
Bihac, 99
Blinken, Antony J., 162–
   3n5
Blue helmet, 170–1n4
'Blue Helmets', 97, 99–100,
   101
   Ogata, 102–3
   Srebrenica massacre,
      103–7
Bosnia, 95, 108, 109, 125
   UNHCR withdrawal,
      102–3
Bosnia-Herzegovina, 3, 33,
   60, 78, 94, 95, 99, 100,
   101, 124, 151, 153–4,
   170–1n4
   Annan, Kofi, 107–9
   detention camp, 3–5
Bosnian Serb forces, 96,
   103–7
Bosnian Serbs, 98
Bouhlel, Ferdaous, 131, 134
Boutros-Ghali, Boutros, 31,
   61, 103, 139
Brahimi, Lakhdar, 113, 116

Brauman, Rony, 68
Brazil, 148, 170–1n4
Bremen, 86
Britain, 73, 96
Brody, Reed, 8
Brussels, 141
Bucha, 153
Bucha, Ukraine, 18, 19
Bugnon, François, 93
Burckhardt, Carl, 86–7, 92
  neutrality, 83–5
Burkina Faso, 127, 136,
  137–8, 140–1
Burundian civil war, 99
Bush administration, 24, 25,
  26, 27, 41–2
Bush, George W., 41, 54
Bybee, Jay S., 26, 27

Cameroon, 127
Camus, Albert, 9–10
Canada, 170–1n4
Carnegie Wateler Peace
  Prize, 124
Catholic Church, 23, 69
Central African Republic,
  127, 154
Centre for Humanitarian
  Dialogue, 7, 48, 116, 120,
  123–4, 138
Chad, 127

Chamberlain, Neville, 19,
  74
Chapuisat, Edouard, 91–2
Charlie-Hebdo (weekly),
  134
Chartier, Christian, 23
Chechnya, 57
Chenevière, Jacques, 92
Chergui, Smaïl, 142
China, 53, 54, 57, 78, 82,
  142–3, 145, 150
  relations, 149
Christian-Democrat party,
  88
Churchill, Winston, 20–21,
  84–5
Churkin, Vitaly, 57
CIA, 25
  ten forms of torture, 26–
  7
Cicero, 22, 24
CMA, 131
Cold War, 13, 67
Cologne, 86
Colombia, 153, 154, 170–
  1n4
compromise vs. complicity,
  68
cosmopolitan law, 24
Côte d'Ivoire, 143
Council of Europe, 121

Covid-19 pandemic, 154
Crane, David, 36, 37,
    160–1n11
Crimea, occupation of, 18,
    39, 113
Crisis Management Initia-
    tive, 48
Croatia, 107
Croatian War of Indepen-
    dence, 170–1n4
Croats, 96
Czech Republic, 170–1n4

Daesh, 114, 116
Dahlerus, Johan Birger
    Essen, 73–4, 98, 166–
    7n10
Damascus, 113, 114, 117,
    119–21
Dar es Salaam, 41
Darfur peace agreement
    (2006), 60
Dayton Accords (1995),
    31, 35, 62, 107
de Maio, Jacques, 101
de Mistura, Staffan, 113,
    115–18, 121
de Soto, Alvaro, 46–7
Democratic Republic of the
    Congo, 148
Denmark, 170–1n4

detention camp: prisoners
    release challenges, 3–5
devil
    categorisations of evil, 28
    image of 22–4
    as terrorist, 24–5
Dicko, Imam Mahmoud,
    137
Diffa region, 139
Dogon, 138, 140
Doha Agreement, 142
Donbas attacks, 18, 39
Drowned and the Saved,
    The (Levi), 9
Dudouet, Véronique, 49–50
Dutch soldiers, 105
Dutch, 161n14

Economic Community of
    West African States
    (ECOWAS), 130
Egypt, xv, xviii, 170–1n4
Eichmann, Adolf, 21, 24
English Channel, 84
Eritrea, 127
Essen, 86
Estonia, 170–1n4
ethics of conviction, 3, 8
'ethics of responsibility', 6,
    7, 8
    risk for mediators, 10–12

Ethiopia, 82, 127
Etter, Philipp, 88–9, 90–1, 92
Europe, 83–4, 87, 96, 107, 127–8, 145, 148, 168n7
European Community (EC), 97, 98–9
European Union (EU), 25, 26, 49, 130–1, 172–3n2
  armed groups, banning of, 41–2
  terrorist organisations lists, 44
  Tuareg rebellion, 128–30
exclusion, 27, 44, 47, 50
Extraordinary African Chambers, 8

Fabius, Laurent, 172–3n2
Farabougou, 140
Finland, 170–1n4
Foulatari, 139
France, 44, 96, 129, 130–2, 143, 161–2n15, 170–1n4
  jihadist groups, 132–6
Free City of Danzig, 84
Free Syrian Army, 121
Freedom House State of Democracy Index, 60–1
French troop, 142
Frick-Cramer, Renée-Marguerite, 89–90

Fulani community, 138–9
Fulani, 133, 138, 140

Gaddafi regime, 57
Gaddafi, Muammar, 38, 175n2
Gaillard, Philippe, 78
Gao region, 138
Gates, Robert, 57
Gaza, 46
Geneva Convention (1929), 82, 86, 88–9, 168–9n9
'Geneva II' conference, 115
Geneva, 83, 97
'genocide', 15, 19, 39, 71, 77, 85, 107–9, 168n7
Georgia and Russia war, 18, 56
German occupation, 168n7
Germanophile, 84
German–Soviet Nonaggression Pact, 10
Germany, 84, 87, 141, 170–1n4
Ghali, 175n2
Ghana, 37, 170–1n4
Ghouta, 114, 123
Global South, 150
Goldstone, Richard, 34, 35, 97
Gorazde, 99

Göring, Hermann, 73–4, 166–7*n*10
Graduate Institute of International Studies, 83
Gramsci, Antonio, 151, 178*n*5
Great Lakes, 95
Greater Sahara, 141
Greek mythology, 13, 29
Gulf of Guinea, 128, 136
Gulf War (1991), 31
Guterres, António, 142, 145–6
Gypsies, 168*n*7

Habré, Hissène, 8
Halifax, Lord, 84
Hamas, xvii–xx, 26, 46–7
  7 October 2023 attack, xvii–xxii
  cease-fire, xviii, xx
Handbook on the Peaceful Settlement of Disputes between States, The, 32
Harland, David, 32, 104, 124
hegemony, *see* Western hegemony; American hegemony
Herceg-Bosna, 5
Herodotus, 29

Hezbollah, 44, 49, 150
High Islamic Council, 140
Hitler, Adolf, 82
Hitlerism, 84
Holbrooke, Richard, 107
Holder v. Humanitarian Law Project (2010), 45–6
Hollande, François, 129
Hollingworth, Larry, 101, 106
Homs, 116
Hôtel Métropole, 89
Huber, Max, 86–8
  on neutrality, 82–3
hubris
  American hubris, 55–6
  fractures the rule of law, 26–8
  a greater sin, 29
Human Rights Quarterly, 34
human selection, 3–4
humanitarian aid, 68, 73, 103, 118, 125
Hurricane Katrina, 56
Hussein, Saddam, 43
Hyper-Cacher, 133–4

Ibogolitan community, 138
Idlib, 123

Idourfan community, 138
'Ikea Peace', 61
impartiality, 70, 72, 77
Inclusive National Dialogue, 136
Independent International Commission of Inquiry, 114, 119
India, 147–8, 170–1n4
Indonesia, 170–1n4
Inquisition, 23
International Commission, 119, 121, 122
International Committee of the Red Cross (ICRC), 6, 15, 33, 77–8
Burckhardt and, 83–5
Etter on, 90–1
Huber and neutrality, 82–3
international law and committee, 85–9
neutrality vs., 81–2
Syria, evacuation, 118–25
International Conference on the Former Yugoslavia, 34–5
International Contact Group, 7
International Criminal Court, 34, 38, 146, 160–1n11

"Articles 16 and 53", 34
"Article 17", 39
international criminal justice, 29–30, 33–4
mandates for mediation, 71
versus the search for peace, 37–40
weaponising, 37–8
International Criminal Tribunal for the former Yugoslavia (ICTY), 6–7, 34, 35, 97, 160n2
International Crisis Group, 141–2
international humanitarian law (IHL), 58–9
Iran, 117, 148
Iranian–Israeli confrontation, 149
Iraq, 147
invasion of (2003), 15, 43, 55
Ireland, 170–1n4
Islam, 135–6
Islamic State, 50, 114
Israel, xvii–xx, 26, 149–50
Israeli–Palestinian conflict, 50
Italian Communist Party, 178n5

Italy, 82, 170–1*n*4

Japan, 82
Jaquemet, Iolanda, 123
Jeune Afrique (weekly), 129
Jews, 86, 87, 168*n*7
jihadists
    agreements, 136–41
    in Sahel, 132–6
    Tuareg rebellion, 128–30
JNIM (Jama'at el nusra wa
    al-islam wa el muslimin),
    134, 140–1
    government troops and
        jihadist groups, 141–4
Jordan, 170–1*n*4
Judeo-Christian culture, 70

Kalashnikovs, 116
Kant, Immanuel, 24, 75
Katzner, Rudolf, 21
Keïta, Ibrahim Boubacar,
    137, 140
Kenya, 170–1*n*4
Khan, Karim, 38–9, 161*n*14
Koro Cercle, 138
kosher supermarket, 133–4
Kosovo conflict, 35, 147
    NATO intervention in,
        55
Kostyuchenko, Elena, 155

Kremlin, 145, 153
Kuwait, 31
Kyiv, 18, 145, 153

Land, Tony, 101, 102
'lawfare', 37
Le Monde (newspaper), 134
League of Nations, 146
League of Nations High
    Commissioner, 84
Lebanon, 44, 150
Lemkin, Raphael, 168*n*7
Levant Front, 121
Levi, Primo, 9
liberal interventionism, 24
liberalism, 31
Liberation Tigers of Tamil
    Eelam (LTTE), 10, 157–
        8*n*6
Libya, 38, 128, 147
    NATO's intervention in,
        57–8
'limited liability partner-
    ships', xx
Lithuania, 170–1*n*4
London, 84
Lord's Resistance Army
    (LRA), 21–2
Luxembourg, 170–1*n*4

Macron, Emmanuel, 17, 19,
    129

Madrid proposal (1933), 168*n*7

Maïga, Abdoulaye Idrissa, 137–8

Malaysia, 170–1*n*4

Malaysian Airlines, 161*n*14

Mali, 28, 49, 127
  agreements, 136–9
  jihadist groups, 132–6
  Tuareg rebellion, 128–30

Mali: Enabling Dialogue with the Jihadist Coalition JNIM (report), 141–2

Manchuria, 82

Mandela, Nelson, 31–2, 98–9

Mariupol, Ukraine, 18, 59

McGinty, Roger, 61

mediation
  American strategy shift, 43
  'the glorious years' of, 32–3
  and humanitarian aid difference, 68
  human rights morality and, 33–7
  ideological marker of the values, 31
  rise of, 32
  risks, 10–12
  See also neutrality

mediators
  avoiding missteps, 75–9
  definition, 70–1
  manipulation of, 73–4
  neutrality and impartiality, 71–2, 77
  resolution 1373 and, 45–6
  role, 31, 33
  strong mediators, 68–9
  symbolic and political power of, 73
  use of, 72–4
  weak mediators, 70, 71–2

Medvedev, Dmitry, 39–40, 57

Ménaka region, 138

Middle Ages, 23

Middle East, 147

Milosevic, Slobodan, 35, 97

minilateralism, xviii, xix

Morawiecki, Mateusz, 17, 18–19

Morocco, 69–70

Moscow, 113, 145

Movement for Unity and Jihad in West Africa (MUJAO), 129

multipolar world, xvii, xx,

xxi, 15, 53, 62, 118, 145, 155

Munich Agreement (1938), 10

Munich Security Conference (2007), 55

Mussolini, Benito, 82, 84

Myanmar, 147

N'Djamena, Chad, 8

N'guelbeli, 139

Nairobi, 41

National Agreement Conference, 136

NATO, 38–9, 96, 98, 99, 128, 161n14
    intervention in Kosovo, 55
    intervention in Libya, 57–8, 111–12
    Srebrenica massacre, 103–7

'Nazism', 147

Nepal, 170–1n4

Netherlands, 161n14, 170–1n4

neutrality, 15, 33, 71–2, 77–8
    Burckhardt on, 83–5
    Huber on, 82–3
    ICRC vs., 81–2

'the new international order', 30–1

New Zealand, 170–1n4

NGOs (mediation), 71–2
    and unofficial mediation, 47–51, 70

Nice, 134

Niger, 127, 136–9

Nigeria, 127, 170–1n4

North Atlantic alliance, 107

Norway, 170–1n4

Norwegian People's Aid (NPA), 46

Nuremberg trials, 73, 74

Obama, Barack, 56, 114, 172–3n2

Ocampo, Luis Moreno, 38

Ogata, Sadako, 102–3, 125

Ohio, 107

Operation Barkhane, 129

Operation Serval, 129

Orford, Anne, 55

Pakistan, 148, 170–1n4

Palestinian Authority, 26, 47

Paris, 141
    jihadist groups, 132–6

Paris, Roland, 61

Pax Americana, 29, 31, 53–63, 111, 117–18, 145

'peace dividend', 30
peace process
  grey zone, 9–10, 12
  peace, redefined, 32
  successive periods, 14–15
'peace versus justice', 34–5
Pearl Harbor, 87
Pictet, Jean, 85
pirates, 22, 23–4
Platform and the Coordination of Azawad Movements130
Poland, 18–19, 170–1n4
Popular Front for the Liberation of Palestine (PFLP), 46, 49
Portugal, 69, 170–1n4
Powell, Jonathan, 50
'practical wisdom', 75–6
Praljak, Slobodan, 7
Prince, The (Machiavelli), 74
Prison Notebooks (Gramsci), 151
private diplomacy, 48–51
Putin, Vladimir, 17, 55–6, 145

Qatar, xvii, xix, xx

Rabbani, Mouin, 118

Račak massacre (Kosovo), 35
Reagan, Ronald, 30
Revolutionary Armed Forces of Colombia (FARC), 44, 49, 153, 162–3n5
Ricard, Philippe, 161–2n15
Richmond, Oliver, 61
Ricoeur, Paul, 20, 68, 75–6, 90, 92, 101
Riegner, Gerhart, 83
Rohingya, 147
Russia, 53, 74, 111–12, 113, 142–3, 145, 147, 149, 150, 161n14
  de Mistura's mediation effort, 115–18
  invasion of Ukraine, 17, 18
  military agreements, 149
  nuclear threat, 17–18, 39–40
  'the responsibility to protect', opposing, 57–8
  support of, 98
  Syrian conflict and, 58, 59, 78–9
Russian air force, 122, 149
Russian army, 57–8

Russian Federation, 170–1*n*4
Russia–Ukraine war, 18–20, 153
    first weeks of, 19
    Western public opinion, 39
Rwanda, 33, 107–8
Rwandan genocide, 77–8

Sahel, 127, 131–2, 151, 152
    agreements, 136–41
    government troops and jihadist groups, 141–4
    jihadist groups, 132–6
    Tuareg rebellion, 128–30
Salafist Group for Preaching and Combat (GSPC), 175*n*2
Salamé, Ghassan, 74
Sarajevo, 102, 104
    UN intervention, 96–100
sarin gas, 114, 123
'Satan II' hypersonic missiles, 17
Saudi Arabia, 149
Scandinavian prisoners, 93
Serbia, 107
Sharia law, 140
Shining Path, 50

Sissi (General), 143
Slovak Republic, 170–1*n*4
Somalia, 31
South Africa, 148
South Sudan, 127
Soviet Union, 30, 168–9*n*9
Spain, 69, 170–1*n*4
Speaking with the 'Bad Guys': Toward Dialogue with Central Mali's Jihadists (report), 142
Srebrenica massacre (1995), 95–6
    Bosnian Serb forces, 103–7
Srebrenica, 95–7, 99, 124
    Annan, Kofi, 107–9
    UN and NATO intervertions, 103–7
Sri Lanka, 157–8*n*6
Sri Lankan army, 10
Stade de France, 134
Stalin, Joseph, 82, 85
Stalingrad, Battle of, 87
Sudan, 154
Sweden, 170–1*n*4
Swedish Red Cross, 93
Swiss Confederation, 88
Switzerland, 82–3, 92, 170–1*n*4
    committee, Etter on, 90–1

international law and
  committee, 85–9
Syria, 15, 33, 57–8, 94, 95,
  111–13, 128, 151
  de Mistura's mediation
    effort, 115–18
  evacuation, 118–25
  mediators, 148–9
  protest, 114
  UN mediation activities,
    78
Syrian artillery, 122

Taliban, 25, 44, 49, 127, 142
  China and, 149
  Tuareg rebellion, 128–30
Talking to Terrorists
  (Powell), 50
Tanzania, 99
Taylor, Charles, 36
terrorist organisations
  exclusion, 47, 50
  international hunt for,
    47–8
  lists, 43–4
  mediation NGOs and,
    48–51
Third Geneva Convention
  (1949), 168–9n9
Third Reich, 82, 85, 86, 93,
  166–7n10

Tillabéry, 138
Togo, Benin, 143
totalitarianism, 28
Transparency International
  Corruption Index, 60–1
Treatment of Prisoners of
  War, 168–9n9
Treaty of Tordesillas (7 Jun
  1494), 69
Treaty of Versailles (1919),
  19
Trump, Donald, 69–70
Tuareg, 131–2
  Tuareg rebellion, 128–30
Tunisia, 170–1n4
Turkey, 117, 147–8, 150,
  170–1n4
  Russia's agreement, 149
Tutsis, 108

Uganda, 21–2, 43
Ukraine, 95, 125, 145, 147,
  150, 155, 161n14, 170–
  1n4
  International Criminal
    Court's activism in,
    38–9
UN High Commissioner
  for Refugees, 102
UN Secretary-General, 154
UN Security Council, 38,

54, 55, 59, 60, 70, 89, 96,
100, 103, 109, 112,
114–15, 116, 129, 131
Annan, 107–9
mediation, 148–54
resolution 1973, 57
resolution 2118, 114–15
resolution 743, 170–1n4
resolution 808, 160n2
resolutions 1373 and
    1267, 41, 42–3, 45–7,
    131
Syria, evacuation, 118–25
United Arab Emirates, 149–
50
United Kingdom (UK),
    170–1n4
United Nations (UN), xvii,
    6, 15, 23, 25, 30–1, 33,
    45, 54, 61–2, 78, 93, 95,
    96–9, 104, 105, 131, 145
Annan, 107–9
compromise to rotten
    compromise, 78
de Mistura's mediation
    effort, 115–18
'democracy' concepts, 59
mediation, 148–54
peace conference, 36–7
'safe areas', 96, 99
Syria, evacuation, 118–25

United Nations High
    Commissioner for
    Refugees (UNHCR),
    100–1
Ogata and, 102–3
Srebrenica massacre,
    103–7
United Nations Multidi-
    mensional Integrated
    Stabilization Mission in
    Mali (MINUSMA), 130
United Nations Protection
    Force (UNPROFOR),
    106, 170–1n4
United States (US), xvii, 57,
    58, 78, 87, 96, 113, 127,
    130–1, 142, 160–1n11,
    170–1n4
erosion of American
    power, 53
helped forge norms, 30–
    1
jihadist groups, 132–6
military intervention in
    Iraq, 54
Putin on US policy, 55–
    6
refused to negotiate with
    Taliban, 25
Russia's agreement, 149

Srebrenica massacre, 103–7
as a strong mediator, 69–70
terrorist organisations' lists, 44
Tuareg rebellion, 128–30
universal jurisdiction, 23–4
'unlawful combatants', 24–5
prisons for, 25
US Office of Foreign Assets Control (OFAC), 45
Uyangoda, Jayadeva, 157–8n6

Viber messaging, 120

Wagner Group, 142
war on terror, 14, 15, 24–5, 53, 67, 127–8, 143, 146–7, 152–3
categorisations of evil, 28
impact on official

mediation, 41, 45–7, 59
ten forms of torture, 26–7
Washington, 84, 98, 113, 114–15
Western hegemony, xix, 14
WhatsApp, 120
World Jewish Congress, 83
World War I, 146, 168–9n9
World War II, 15, 19, 33, 77, 78, 81, 93, 151
end of, 95–6
UN intervention, 96–100

Yugoslavia, 31, 33, 35, 95, 99, 101, 103, 160n2, 170–1n4

Zagreb, 98
Zelensky, Volodymyr, 19–20, 145–6
Zepa, 99